My Bread

THE REVOLUTIONARY NO-WORK, NO-KNEAD METHOD

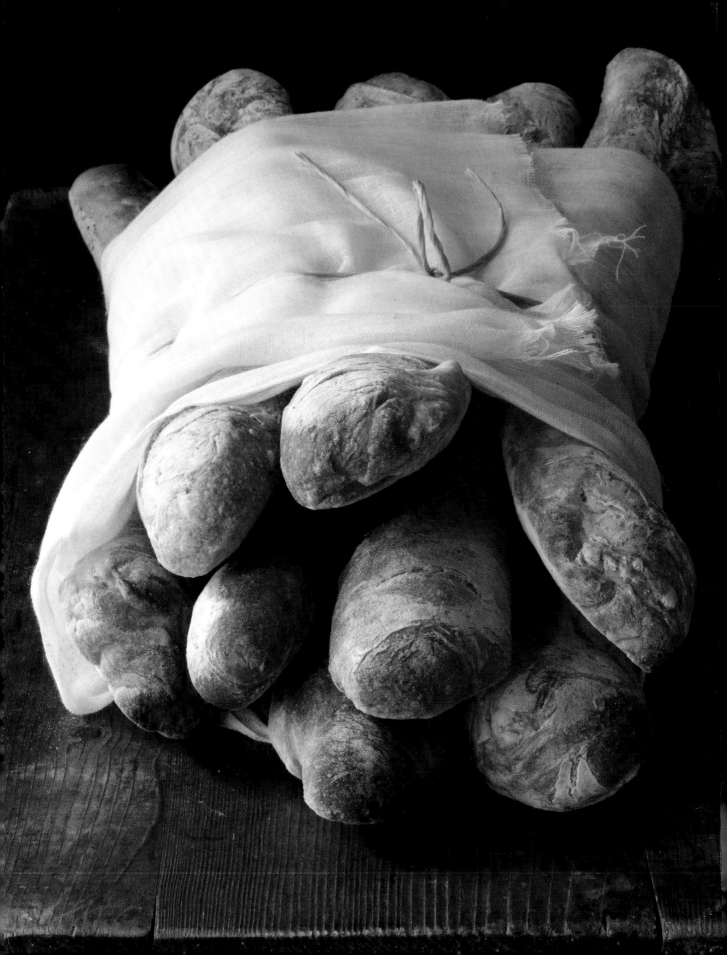

My Bread

THE REVOLUTIONARY NO-WORK, NO-KNEAD METHOD

Jim Lahey

Founder of the
Sullivan Street Bakery

with Rick Flaste

Photographs by Squire Fox

W. W. Norton & Company
New York London

For information about permission to reproduce selections from this book,
write to Permissions, W. W. Norton & Company, Inc.,
500 Fifth Avenue, New York, NY 10110

For information about special discounts for bulk purchases, please contact
W. W. Norton Special Sales at specialsales@wwnorton.com or 800-233-4830

Manufacturing by The Courier Companies, Inc.
Book design by Studio 421
Production manager: Andrew Marasia

Library of Congress Cataloging-in-Publication Data

Lahey, Jim.
    My bread : the revolutionary no-work, no-knead method / Jim Lahey,
with Rick Flaste ; photographs by Squire Fox.
    p. cm.
    Includes index.
    ISBN 978-0-393-06630-2 (hardcover)
1. Bread. I. Flaste, Richard. II. Title.
    TX769.L256 2009
    641.8'15—dc22

                                                    2009017356

W. W. Norton & Company, Inc.
500 Fifth Avenue, New York, N.Y. 10110
www.wwnorton.com

W. W. Norton & Company Ltd.
Castle House, 75/76 Wells Street, London W1T 3QT

    3 4 5 6 7 8 9 0

To my mother, Cecilia, who indulged me so caringly throughout my childhood, and also to my wife, Anitha, for all her love.

Contents

Acknowledgments 13

Introduction 15

CHAPTER 1: **The Making of a Bread Baker** 19

Using My Hands: The First Loaf 20

Italy: The Art of Bread 22

San Gimignano: Bread from the Earth 23

BOX: Brick-Oven Baking in San Gimignano 24

Brooklyn: Baking for Money, Sometimes 25

Manhattan: Real Work 26

Rome: The Baker's Life 28

Genzano: The Aesthetic of Bread 29

Sullivan Street: An Italian Bakery in New York 31

Less Is More: No-Knead Bread 33

CHAPTER 2: **The Lahey Method for No-Knead Bread in a Pot** 37

THE MIRACLE—HOW IT HAPPENS 39

Flour, Water, and Time 39

Yeast and Salt 40

Heat 41

An Oven Within an Oven—The Pot 42

BOX: Singing 47

Weighing Your Options 48

A Note on Bread Flour 48

Storing Bread 49

THE BASIC NO-KNEAD BREAD RECIPE 50

CHAPTER 3: **Specialties of the House**   57

Pane Integrale • Whole Wheat Bread   61

Rye Bread   63

Pan co' Santi • Walnut Bread   66

Pane all'Olive • Olive Bread   69

Pane con Formaggio • Cheese Bread   71

Pancetta Bread   73

VARIATION: PANCETTA ROLLS   74

Stecca • Stick or Small Baguette   77

VARIATION: STECCA POMODORI, ALL'OLIVE, O AL'AGLIO
(STECCA WITH TOMATOES, OLIVES, OR GARLIC)   78

Stirato • Italian Baguette   79

Ciabatta • Slipper Loaf   81

Coconut-Chocolate Bread   85

Banana Leaf Rolls   87

Jones Beach Bread   90

VARIATION: OCEAN BREAD WITH NORI   91

BEYOND WATER (BEER, JUICES, AND MORE)   92

Jim's Irish Brown Bread   93

VARIATION: IRISH BROWN BREAD WITH CURRANTS   94

Carrot Bread   97

Apple Bread   99

Peanut Bread   101

Peanut Butter and Jelly Bread   105

Almond-Apricot Bread   108

Fresh Corn Bread   110

Fennel-Raisin Bread   112

CHAPTER 4:   **Pizzas and Focaccias**   115

Basic Pizza Dough   117
Pizza Pomodoro • Tomato Pizza   120
VARIATION: PIZZA AMATRICIANA (TOMATO PIZZA WITH PANCETTA AND ONION)   121
BOX: Slicing Pizza   122
BOX: The Thin Slice   122
Pizza Funghi • Mushroom Pizza   126
Pizza Cavolfiore • Cauliflower Pizza   128
Pizza Patate • Potato Pizza   129
VARIATION: PIZZA BATATA (SWEET POTATO PIZZA)   130
Pizza Zucchine • Zucchini Pizza   132
Pizza Radici di Sedano • Celery Root Pizza   133
Pizza Cipolla • Onion Pizza   134
Pizza Bianca   137
VARIATION: SCHICCIATA D'UVA (SWEET RAISIN AND GRAPE PIZZA)   139
Pizza Finocchio • Fennel Pizza   140
Focaccia   141
Focaccia Dolce • Sweet Focaccia   144

CHAPTER 5:   **The Art of the Sandwich**   147

HOMEMADE SANDWICH INGREDIENTS   150
Rosemary Roast Beef   150
Citrus Roast Pork   152
BOX: How to Tie a Roast   154
Jim's Aioli   156
Homemade Pickles   157
Homemade Spicy Mustard   158
Artichoke Confit   159
Marinated Eggplant   160
Marinated Beets   162

Marinated Sun-Dried Tomatoes 164

Roasted Red Peppers 165

Spicy Eggplant Spread 166

Lemon Dressing 167

Green Onion Bagna Cauda

• Green Onion, Anchovy, and Garlic Sauce 168

VARIATION: RAMP BAGNA CAUDA 169

Frittata Patate • Potato Omelette 170

PANINI (THE SANDWICHES) 172

Panino di Manzo • Roast Beef Sandwich with Aioli 173

Panino Cubano • Cuban Sandwich 174

Panino di Carciofi e Prosciutto Cotto

• Artichoke and Ham Sandwich 176

Panino di Caprese • Mozzarella and Tomato Sandwich 177

Panino di Melanzane

• Eggplant Sandwich with Roasted Red Pepper 178

Panino di Mozzarella

• Mozzarella Sandwich with Eggplant Spread 179

Panino di Bresaola • Dried Beef Sandwich with Arugula 180

Panino di Barbietola • Beet Sandwich with Goat Cheese 181

Panino "PMB" • Pancetta, Mango, and Basil Sandwich 182

The "Rampwich" • Green Onion Bagna Cauda,

Mozzarella, and Duck Egg Sandwich 184

The "Speckeroni" • Speck with Pecorino Sandwich 185

Panino Frittata • Omelette Sandwich 186

CHAPTER 6: **Stale Bread** 189

Panzanella • Bread Salad 192

Pappa al Pomodoro • Tomato Bread Soup 194

Gazpacho 196

Ribollita • Thick Tuscan Bean and Kale Soup 198

Tomato Bruschetta 200

VARIATION: NEAPOLITAN TOMATO BRUSCHETTA 201

Roasted Red Pepper Bruschetta 202

Budino • Bread Pudding Tart 204

BOX: Bruna's Pasta Frolla 207

Tortino di Cioccolato • Chocolate Torte 209

Homemade Bread Crumbs 211

Index 213

Acknowledgments

This is my first book, and it required many talented people to lead me all the way from start to finish. I'm incredibly grateful to all of them.

Maria Guarnaschelli, my editor at W. W. Norton, was the guiding hand throughout the project. Janis Donnaud, our agent, brought Rick Flaste and me together as writing partners and now friends, too. Mark Bittman, with his *Minimalist* column in the *New York Times,* provided my new baking technique with its initial boost in print and gave it life around the world.

An immense thank you goes to Lillian Chou, a former *Gourmet* food editor who tirelessly tested recipes, with assistance from Shelley Wiseman.

Those on my staff, past and present, whose organizational abilities made it possible for me to survive hectic days of recipe creation, running a bakery, and starting a restaurant, include Colleen Duffy, Anatte Litvak, and Jada Gorrell. Two other assistants, in addition to proving themselves invaluable in the office, also added skillful aid in creating the recipes: Amanda McDougal and Fayth Preyer. Contributing their cooking talents to the project were Lauren Furman and Jeff Gossett. Joining in at key points with their well-honed editorial skills were Zoe Singer, Jaimee Young, and Ana Deboo.

Among those who stood with me as my baking career evolved in the early days were Joe Allen, who financed many of my efforts, especially the first Sullivan Street Bakery, and my former business partner Monica Von Thun Calderon.

At Norton, working with Maria Guarnaschelli, there was an impressive team: Bill Rusin, sales director; Louise Brockett, publicity director; Susan Sanfrey, project editor; Nancy Palmquist, managing editor; Ingsu Liu, art director; Andrew Marasia, head of production; Adrian Kitzinger, layout artist; Sue Carlson, digital production manager; and the indispensable Melanie Tortoroli, editorial assistant.

So much of the visual beauty in this book is the work of the splendid photographer, Squire Fox, and his assistant, David Sullivan. The prop stylist was Nan Whitney and the food stylist Kevin Crafts. Tricia Joyce was the agent for photography and Jann Johnson the producer who helped coordinate that effort.

Also playing a major role in creating the handsome appearance of the book was Jan Derevjanik, its designer.

Although less directly involved, I want to express a heartfelt thank you to some great friends who offered me a place to stay when I lived and worked in Italy and also when I returned to refresh my memory in the service of this book: Allesandra L'Abate, Renato Baldisserotto, Giovanni and Johanna L'Abate, and Michael Coleman.

And, more broadly, I want to extend my deepest gratitude to the people of Italy and all the bakers I ever met there for their warmth and their inspirational appreciation of wonderfully crafted bread.

Introduction

Though I couldn't have anticipated it, I'm flattered and delighted—blown away, really—by the worldwide and seemingly never-ending attention my no-knead, bread-in-a-pot technique has received since the recipe was published in the *New York Times* in November 2006. The article, written by Mark Bittman, had an immediate impact: a cascade of Internet traffic that resulted in home bakers all around the world giving it a shot—and reporting great success. Through television, print media, and blogs, the Lahey method has taken on a powerful life of its own.

That's just what I always wanted. I wanted to do whatever I could to help bread matter more, for people to fall in love with bread as I did when I began baking two decades ago. The object of my deepest affection, especially early on, was always the rustic, deep-flavored bread of the Italian countryside.

I am (I admit it) a driven man—driven by the belief that bread, especially the mass-produced bread we find most everywhere, no longer enjoys the respect it once had. And, unfortunately, most of the better bread made in this country can only be found in boutique bakeries, often located too far away from home, and for too much money. Also, to my mind, so many of the so-called artisanal breads are the result of shortcuts and compromises. We don't have a strong bread culture in America. Too many people don't really know what bread should taste like, and too few have experienced the process of baking it. For most people, the best way to taste bread as it should be is to bake it themselves.

Good bread should be a masterpiece of contrast, crackling as you bite through the browned, malty-smelling crust, then deeply satisfying as you get to the meaty, chewy crumb with its distinct wheaten, slightly acidic taste. And that's precisely the sort of loaf you'll produce at home with my method. It relies on only flour, water, salt, and a tiny amount of yeast, with very little in the way of effort or equipment. The recipe is so simple and forgiving it's practically foolproof.

I start this book with my own story—The Making of a Bread Baker—which I hope you'll find both instructive and a good read. In Chapter 2, we get to the technique itself, which I arrived at after years of experimentation. The technique is simply this: the dough is lightly mixed and allowed to rise very slowly for 12 to 18 hours (there is no vigorous kneading), then baked in a preheated pot that serves as an oven within an oven. In that chapter, I also spell out the chemistry and other details of the miracle that turns a gluey mess into something beyond terrific.

In the following chapter, I offer variations on my master recipe, each with its own distinct appeal, from an olive-studded loaf to an Italian baguette (the *stirato*). You'll find some playfulness here, too, with several unusual breads like the ones that use juice as the liquid instead of water. All along the way, I encourage you to experiment, to find your own variations. There's also a chapter on bread's closest cousin, pizza, and one on Italian sandwiches, which I think may surprise you as you come to understand how much thought can go into the pairing of ingredients with great bread. And since I hope you'll be baking bread more and more (and so will have a lot left over), I included recipes in the final chapter that illustrate how to take stale bread and bring it back to life in exciting dishes. The possibilities for gustatory satisfaction and personal fulfillment are endless.

CHAPTER 1

The Making of a Bread Baker

USING MY HANDS: THE FIRST LOAF

I baked bread for the first time to impress a girl. I was in college, at the State University of New York at Stony Brook. An aspiring painter and sculptor, I was driven to be different from everybody else in every way, to be unforgettably impressive—if I could figure out how. (I had already become obsessed with cooking, studying Anne Willan's *La Varenne Pratique*, because I couldn't stand cafeteria food.) What gift would I bring this young woman? Something I could make, something from my own hands. Baking struck me as the right idea. Bread's sculptural quality attracted me. I don't think anybody else I knew then, crazy as some of them were, would imagine that thrusting a loaf at his girlfriend was the most romantic idea in the world. It was very definitely unusual as gifts go.

I set out to impress with simplicity, with a particularly basic Italian white bread. I don't recall much about how that first loaf looked and tasted, but all these years later I still remember the girl's reaction clearly. First she was taken aback, and then warmly flattered. I got the sense that she thought I was a little nuts, which wasn't far from the mark.

Once the baking inspiration struck, I realized it wasn't going to be a one-shot sort of thing: it suited me wonderfully, partly for psychological reasons. My mind is always in a bit of hyperactive turmoil, and the emotional escape bread baking brings, with its required focus and intensity, can push everything else away. While I was baking, I felt none of the inadequacy and uncertainty that otherwise accompanied me in college or my brief tenure at the School of Visual Arts in New York. I slowly became something of a bread scholar, starting, as I recall, with James Beard's *Beard on Bread* and then going on to create a bread library that went beyond recipes to history and chemistry.

Baking had other rewards beyond the psychological and cerebral: I loved getting messy, flour flying, dough sticking to my hands and clothes. I reveled in the tactile joy of baking bread—so much of which was like working with clay. When it was all over, I was

thrilled that not only could my creation be appreciated as an object, the way sculpture is, but that it would be consumed, internalized by someone I cared about. I wanted to give bread to lots of people. Later I began to be paid for baking, but even now, whether I give the bread away or sell it, the happiness is still there for me.

ITALY: THE ART OF BREAD

My initial interest in bread was incidental to other aspects of my life. While I was still in school, I had the life-altering inspiration to go to Rome. As an artist, I needed to visit the font of the world's great art, and as a student, I had a language requirement to fulfill, which was going to take practice. I did both during a vacation of just a couple of weeks in 1986, traveling with a group from Stony Brook. But even there, although bread had nothing to do with my main objectives, I was drawn to baking. I began haunting bakeries, savoring chewy, flour-dusted round rolls as I walked through the ancient Roman ruins; lining up with schoolchildren for slices of freshly made *pizza bianca* sold by the length; and generally having the eye-opening experience that strikes so many Americans on their first trip to Europe. I joined the other tourists checking out churches and frescoes, going to the markets. I had never before tasted tomatoes so sweet you could eat them like a peach. I'd never seen swallows dance in the sky.

In retrospect, my first trip to Italy was a fateful one. It was to be followed by several return visits during the early '90s, when I was in my mid-twenties (and later too), each more focused than the last on the art of baking. Bread was a magnet for me, an irresistible fascination that would become my life.

Cooking, of course, mattered in Rome, but it was a particular kind of cooking—not fancy, no culinary showing off. It was basic and traditional, the reason that grandmothers in the kitchen are so admired there. You could create real beauty with fresh, simple ingredients and careful preparation. I came home from that first trip not only speaking better Italian and knowing a lot more about art history, but also having learned that I needed to cook as well as bake (the skill of cooking would serve me well much later, as you'll see in the chapter on sandwiches, where I cook from scratch to fill loaves I've baked).

I dove into cookbooks, emerging as a disciple of Carol Field's *The Italian Baker*, from which I made rough country-style loaves of bread that couldn't have had less in common with the soft white stuff sold as "Italian bread" in New York. (It's still stocked at a supermarket near you—I suppose it has its place for some reason.) When I left the School of Visual Arts (expelled, actually, which is hard to manage there), my dad hired me at his printing shop in SoHo, where I had about as much responsibility as most recent students and was soon bored out of my skull. All I wanted to do was go back to Italy, and the minute I, and my girlfriend at the time, Eileen, had saved enough money, we were on a plane to Rome.

SAN GIMIGNANO: BREAD FROM THE EARTH

We spent eight months in San Gimignano, in Tuscany, working and living at a cooperative farm and vineyard. The residents there, some of them artsy, vagrant types like us, tended the vines and harvested the grapes. Inevitably, I ended up in the kitchen and sometimes outside at the wood-burning oven. My breads began to have the rustic look I'd seen there and in Rome. They developed a deeper-colored crust, a more open crumb, and a richer flavor.

I felt extraordinarily free in San Gimignano, both in spirit and thought. It was the sort of place—remote, peaceful, and beautiful—that gave me the emotional strength to develop my own ideas about baking and about life. The town lies above the Val d'Orcia, one of the most fertile places in Tuscany, bathed in that romanticized sun, a constant, gentle light. Well before the birth of the Roman Empire, the Etruscans (from whom the name Tuscany comes) were there, clearing the forests in that expansive valley to grow wheat, still a principal crop in the area. I gained a deep appreciation for agriculture there that has stayed with me. That experience is one reason why when I smell a loaf of good bread, I always feel so close to the wheat itself.

BRICK-OVEN BAKING IN SAN GIMIGNANO

When I worked on the Tuscan farm in the '90s, I got pretty good at using the wood-burning brick oven next to the house. It's a lot more difficult—if more authentically traditional—than the method I teach in this book.

On a recent trip to Italy, I returned to spend a couple of nights at the San Gimignano farmhouse in Tuscany, to see my great friend Michael, who lives there full-time and my friends Gianni and Kristina, who stay there on the weekends. And I really wanted to use that oven again, this time with my no-knead, long-rising dough.

I just love the feeling of the process, that muscular sense of getting the oven ready. A lot came back to me as I got the dough mixed and fermenting, then fired up the oven with armfuls of cut gnarled grapevines that had been drying beautifully in an unruly pile at the edge of the woods. As with any other fire, you start small and keep building until the fire is blazing and self-sustaining. Seeing the ceiling of the oven turn white with heat is one indication that the fireplace is very hot. Then you take a rake or a trowel and spread the embers evenly across the floor of the oven to heat the whole enclosure. You leave those embers there for about a half hour before raking them out, and then you quickly sweep the ashes off the floor so it is clean and ready for baking.

As I did all this, I worried that I'd been too timid and hadn't made a strong enough fire to give me really tremendous heat. But I pressed on, hoping that it would work. I shaped the dough. I told myself maybe this would be decent bread after all. I used a peel to shovel in the shaped loaves as quickly as I was able, so as not to let out too much heat through the open door. But my fears were justified. It had been a long time since I'd done this, and my fire had been inadequate. The bread didn't bake thoroughly, emerging pale and doughy, and a sense of failure swept over me.

Then Michael, tooling up the unpaved road to the farmhouse on his bike, came to the rescue. He is a truly astonishing guy. He's a stonemason, a linguist, a trained masseur, an oboe player, a bassist—and one of the best bakers I know. We decided to wipe away my earlier failure and begin again. We prepared new dough, using some of the remnants, already fermented and thus yeast-rich, from the previous batch.

This promising new batch would be left to ferment overnight, but I was nervous about how erratic the Tuscan nights are. They can be cool or warm, and the temperature affects the growth of the yeast. If it's too cold, the fermentation period has to be longer; too warm, it needs to be shorter. Baking at home, with a room temperature of around 72 degrees Fahrenheit, is just about right for an overnight rise. In professional bakeries, bakers figure out precisely what effect the ambient temperature will have and adjust the temperature of the water mixed into the flour. In the cool conditions we happened to find ourselves in this time in Tuscany, with no way to measure the exact temperature of the air or water, we just hoped for the best.

When I awoke in the predawn, Michael was already working on the fire, piling on the wood, forcing it together with a trowel and creating an infernal blaze that made my attempt the day before look puny. Once the stove was so hot it was difficult to be near, he pulled the embers out with broad, deep, graceful movements. Then we added the loaves. This time they baked through, emerging with a spectacular dark crust.

BROOKLYN: BAKING FOR MONEY, SOMETIMES

Back home, full of thoughts about baking but floundering, I moved to Williamsburg, Brooklyn, a place I could afford (sort of) with no real plans. It was the early '90s; I was in my twenties.

I was feeling pretty grim about my prospects and just trying to get by. But gradually, as I moved from job to job to make the rent, I began to settle into serious baking, again those rustic, crusty loaves. I had enough energy, that's for sure, and you don't need money or anything fancy to bake bread, just hands and an oven. Flour, water, and yeast cost as close to nothing as ingredients can get. It wouldn't occur to me for some time that bread could be a full-time career, but it was becoming an undeniable, growing passion.

Willamsburg was still a neighborhood under the radar, with the feel of an industrial backwater. Eileen and I lived in a number of semihabitable rentals in the area, but the one that is clearest in my mind and most pivotal in my development as a baker was on North 8th Street. It was a converted truck garage with a makeshift bathroom, the kind of place only dysfunctional kids or others barely making it would ever dream of calling home. I set about finding tenants to share the rent. Mostly they, like me, looked for odd jobs to survive. The garage had a large aluminum door in the middle to accommodate a truck and two ordinary doors on either side. Above one was a crawl space about four or five feet high, meant to be a cramped office or storage area. That's where Eileen and I slept. Below us was a minimal kitchen with an electric stove, where I soon began turning out enough bread to sell in the neighborhood.

I baked Italian-style loaves as I had in San Gimignano, and with their sweet wheat flavor and crackling brown crusts, they had a handcrafted, freshly made appeal that seemed out of the ordinary in those days. I took to loading my breads into a big wicker basket and taking them, along with a little folding card table, on the subway to a street market in SoHo. I'd sell focaccia for $1.25 each and big loaves of bread for $2.50. What I couldn't sell, I'd give away. It was a strange practice. I'd walk into a bar with my unsold bread and just give it to people who were willing enough to take it. Some would look at me strangely, a skinny kid bearing home-baked loaves. "Here, try it—it's good stuff, man."

MANHATTAN: REAL WORK

Of course, I wasn't earning a living from that card table, and I seemed to be continually starting a new day job. I counted once, and in a single year I had thirty-seven different jobs. Some were food-related—I was a prep cook, chopping vegetables, at a couple of restaurants—but most, like the one as a salesman at a button shop and another at a stationery warehouse, were just where I ended up thanks to the classifieds. After a while, unsurprisingly, I found myself wanting steadier, more meaningful work. So I figured I'd apply at one or another of the new "artisanal-style" bakeries—meaning they used less machinery and paid more attention to quality than commercial factories.

Artisanal baking had suddenly become big business in the early 1990s, and I stuck my nose into a number of the bakeries that were well regarded at the time for their more sophisticated, European-style breads. To my dismay, none were bustling with happy workers turning out golden loaves of leaven heaven. Instead, like so many of the places where I'd held menial jobs, the work seemed to be mostly done by uncaring, often unskilled employees.

Amy's Bread seemed different. Amy Scherber had a solid French culinary background. She'd opened her place in Hell's Kitchen in 1992 and quickly met with acclaim. I didn't have a résumé to offer her, of course, so I just called. "Can I bring you a loaf of bread?" I asked. "Sure," she said, "why not?" I showed up with one of my loaves of white Italian bread. We met in an aromatic little kitchen where anise, raisins, and herbs infused the air. I slapped my loaf on the table, and she sniffed it knowingly, tasted it . . . and asked me when I could start.

Initially things went wonderfully. I shaped the dough, chopped prosciutto, cleaned rosemary, and the like. Amy had a small crew. One woman handled recipes and did the mixing before I got to the shaping of the dough. Another did the baking. The operation was focused on quality in a way that I could believe in. But my stint here, like everywhere else I'd worked thus far, was short. I just couldn't seem to fit into the pattern; I didn't get along with my coworkers, and one day I announced I wasn't going to stay.

I mention my time at Amy's not to show myself continuing to stumble along, or to knock the bakery, which I admired, but because it was at that point in my life that I began to see possibilities. I'd become increasingly passionate about the dignity of bread and baking. Bread in most of America had become so degraded, and I found I wanted to be one of the missionaries who would lead it back to a position of pride, something to be honored.

As I had that first day at Amy's, I started showing up at restaurants with bags of bread, talking to the chefs and owners, and, in my impassioned way, beginning to sound as if I knew what I was talking about. Or maybe the bread sold itself. I was hired to bake at Orso, an Italian restaurant on West 46th Street owned by the restaurateur Joe Allen and run by his kids, Julie and Ray. My unusually robust loaves were well matched to the high-quality but unpretentious menu there.

The kitchen at Orso fostered my growth by providing me with the resources to create the kind of rugged, flavorful breads I'd discovered in Italy. And when I began to feel that I'd taught myself as much as I could by reading and experimenting and that the next logical step would be to return to the bakeries of Italy, the Allens agreed, sending me back to Rome and to nearby Genzano, famed for its enormous, rustic loaves. This time I would be there purely as a student of bread.

ROME: THE BAKER'S LIFE

As soon as I arrived in Rome, this ancient city that I knew had once revered bread more than any other, and which still cares a great deal about it, I set out to visit the best bakery in town, a place I'd learned about during my time in San Gimignano. It wasn't hard to find the Forno Campo de Fiori. It's in the heart of Rome and known throughout the city. The moment I set foot inside, I felt it: the sense of bread as a treasured thing, an object of honor, as it must have been everywhere before the Industrial Revolution led to mass production. The bakery itself was a lively, invigorating place, and it took me in. It was there that I learned how fulfilling day-to-day life at a wonderful, professional bakery could be.

The Forno was a perfect place to study the mixing of the dough, the cutting, shaping, and baking of it—and to see how it could be done in harmony and well. The bakery is a warren of small rooms, and the bakers need to move about with an orchestrated grace to avoid bumping into each other. A good deal of the show is visible from the plaza. It's part of the charm of the place. People dining at outdoor tables at the trattoria next door, for instance, can look directly into the room where an old man dimples (creating mounds and wells in the dough) and bakes pizza while a young apprentice grates cheese.

I was proud to be there. One of the most memorable things about the place is that those great Roman bakers were pretty happy to be doing what they were doing, and they cared about it. As I'd learned, in too many American bakeries, baking often just seems like something people do to survive. When I've revisited the Forno, the contrast is reinforced by how many of the same faces I see there all these years later. (It helps, of course, that they have tremendous job security, an Italian tradition.)

One of the oldest bakers stands at a steel table cutting and weighing dough for loaves. Years of experience have taught his hands exactly what the dough should feel like as it is shaped. Incredibly, just about every piece of dough he throws on the scale is the exact same weight. Maybe once in ten times he does what I've witnessed so often (and do myself frequently enough): cuts off another piece of dough and adds it to the lump on the scale to get the weight just right.

Dino Bartocci, one of the Forno's partners and founders (the bakery opened in 1970), is still there. On my last visit, I noticed that he'd had his terrible teeth replaced with a brand-new smile, which he shows off every chance he gets. (Goes wonderfully with that shock of white hair.) Dino recalls that, despite my ragtag looks, I was alert back then and picking up what was going on in the bakery, but he admits that he never imagined I would get very far. He credits my success to what he now graciously calls my tenacity—the boneheaded obsessiveness that brought a scruffy, sleep-deprived kid back to the bakery night after night.

Maximo, a gangly man who sells the breads by weight up front in the retail area, likes to remind me of how bedraggled I was then, when I would show up every night at midnight to join the nighttime crew and help out however they'd let me. Then there's Fabrizio, another partner, who is massively built with dark, hairy arms; he's balding and convivial but also gruff and, like a lot of Romans, he can seem dismissively blasé. The last time I was there, I brought him a loaf from Sullivan Street, and he sniffed it and nodded, muttering, "Bread is bread." But when he visited my bakery in New York a month or so later, he was full of compliments and wished the Forno could take the time to let its bread ferment longer before baking so it would taste like mine. Wow, that was a nice thing to hear.

GENZANO: THE AESTHETIC OF BREAD

From Rome, on that trip financed by Orso, I traveled to Genzano, an important pilgrimage for any aspiring baker. If working at the Forno showed me how well a bakery could run and how much satisfaction it could bring both the customers and the bakers, the bakeries of Genzano are where I found loaf after loaf of the kind of bread I'd been striving to achieve. It was here that I learned more than anywhere else about what I call the aesthetic of bread: the look, taste, and technique that I would carry home with me.

Genzano is in a castle-dotted region south of Rome, with wide views of mountains, and the town is packed with bakeries. The brick oven is revered with an intensity that you don't find many other places. Huge, with arched openings and solid metal doors, these great ovens are not built just for looks. Though they predate gas and require a lot of labor in gathering the fuel (hardwoods, like cherry and apple), they produce a powerful heat and, more subtly, impart just the slightest bit of additional flavor to the bread, a smokiness almost, that's easy to miss if you're not looking for it. The people of Genzano like their crusts darker than the Romans do; the flavor of the bread is stronger, slightly acrid, in part because of that near-burnt crust.

You can see the influence of Genzano bread most in the huge oval *filones* that I bake at Sullivan Street and in my basic no-knead bread-in-a-pot recipe (page 50)—the darkness of the crust is the signature. When it is sliced, the interior of the bread, the crumb as it is known, has holes of varying sizes, usually somewhere between a dime and a quarter, a product of the gas in the yeast-produced fermentation and the amount of water in the dough. Bread this good doesn't need to be embellished with oil or butter. It can be enjoyed for its own sake, a satisfying study in counterpoint between the crackling crust and the meaty, slightly sweet crumb.

Genzano is one of three towns in Italy with the right to label its bread with the country's official designation guaranteeing origin, the IGP, or *Indicazione Geografica Protetta* (the other two towns that share bragging rights are Alto Mura in Apulia and Terni in Umbria). The designation is a guarantee of quality, of the care the bakers take in producing their rustic-style bread.

The bakery where I spent most of my time was the Forno a Legna da Sergio, run by Mafalda, the matriarch, an old lady who would frequently sit out front in her apron. Inside you'd find Sergio, the head baker and an owner, a convivial man, happy about his work and his place in the world. He'd pull eighty loaves at a time from the floor of the blazing brick oven, each with a deeply browned crust, hissing and crackling as it cooled.

In addition to breads, the shop sells a spectacular array of biscotti and tarts, including a favorite of mine, the flourless bitter almond tart. But bread has always been the focus. The bakers' affection for it was apparent not only in how they baked, but in how they spoke. In an effusive moment, Sergio once sang out that you had to "caress the dough like the thighs of a woman." Nevertheless, they knead their dough vigorously, beating it up much more than I do these days.

SULLIVAN STREET: AN ITALIAN BAKERY IN NEW YORK

When I came back to Orso, I was restless. It wasn't long before I needed to be on my own. My employers could sense it too, and they encouraged me to give it a try. After all, I could still provide them with my breads, if I baked them elsewhere. I was hoping for a job as a consultant or to start my own bakery. Nothing permanent came up immediately, so I baked around wherever I could for a while, most importantly working on my own in the predawn at a welcoming place called Bruno's in Williamsburg. It was owned by the Settepanni twins, Biagio and Nino. (I have to mention that their name means "seven breads," if you can believe it.)

But soon, with Joe Allen's backing, I opened the Sullivan Street Bakery. In 1994, it wasn't the gleaming shop it would become a few years later, with a long glass display case and all the usual products of an Italian bakery like the Forno in Genzano: sandwich offerings, coffee, tarts. It started out as a rough-hewn place, with a butcher-block counter in front and the bakery itself behind. You might see loaves of bread cooling in big plastic laundry baskets (I still use these). But early on there were no customers to speak of, just a couple of restaurant clients and the occasional passerby. Yet I'd come a long way to get there. I still seemed like the same guy: a wiry bohemian with an erratic, somewhat hyper personality whose primary fashion statement was a thick coat of flour adhering to ratty shorts and a T-shirt (most bakers look god-awful most of the time—it's a messy business). But I'd grown up.

I had an apartment on Spring Street, literally steps away from the shop. From the very beginning, I was determined never to overstretch myself with too many offerings—the sure path to mediocrity—and, of course (no surprise), I was determined to be unique. My *pane pugliese* was the basic loaf at Sullivan Street. Though it's named for Apulia, on the Adriatic heel of Italy, the bread is pretty much my own creation. Most of the bakers I met in Rome were from Apulia, and so, in a way, it honors them. There's also some Genzano in it: I wanted that fermented, slightly acrid taste, that nearly burnt look, a kind of bread that I didn't see in New York City or anywhere in America then.

Of course I couldn't just plop some ovens into the Sullivan Street shop and start selling. I had to practice, even after all the baking I'd already done. This was the first time—as, finally, an owner and a retailer—that my own name and skills were so completely on the line. I was striving for the perfect bread, an image, my ideal. In the oven, I used to have the loaves "kiss," that is, touch each other at the ends, so that the heat wasn't so harsh there that it would create the typical hard heel you can't bite into. It seems like a small thing, but the difference is impressive.

I fired up the ovens at Sullivan Street for the first time when I turned twenty-eight on June 6, 1994. But I didn't formally open until September 15, after I spent a long, hot summer sweating the small stuff. At first a former schoolmate named Rob worked with me. Soon we were joined by Rich, a young bartender who had never baked but needed a job. Rich was a long-haired punk-rocker sort of guy who liked to say "dude" a lot, and the music in that bakery, blasting in the wee hours (Nick Cave and the Bad Seeds, the Ramones) set the tone in more ways than one. The driving rhythm was perfect for long hours of hard, crazy work that didn't end until dawn. Those early days were frantic: three of us baking huge quantities of *pane pugliese*. The work is exhausting, especially before you build up your stamina. Hands and arms fly as you mix the dough, cut it, shape it, hurl it along the floured table. Flour permeates everything; it's on the floor, your body, in the air, even if you can't see it.

At this point, I hadn't turned yet to the no-knead approach; I was still beating the hell out of the dough under the conventional impression that it would be strengthened that way. And I was struggling with the problem inherent in all artisanal baking: consistency. There is something almost irreconcilable about trying to make a bread by hand in the artisan fashion, staying away from machines as much as you can, while producing the identical, predictable thing over and over again, so that a buyer can be sure about exactly what's going to arrive on the truck. When I smell bread and taste it, then as now, I'm often filled with frustration. I'll knock on a loaf, and fail to hear that telltale little echo that tells me the bread has expanded properly.

Even now at the bakery, I often stop working to cut open my loaves and try, succeeding at gentleness only sometimes, to point out to my bakers where one loaf is too dense, another undercooked, a third poorly shaped. Times like those can make anyone understand why people invented factories, where everything comes out the same. And it's times like these when you have to be willing to look at some loaves that didn't make it and just say, "Dump them."

I sold many of the first breads from Sullivan Street in much the way I had in Williamsburg. I'd head out into the street and try to get some money for a loaf. Failing that, I'd give the bread away. People tended to think the bread was a mistake. I know that seems weird now, when the rustic Italian bread I was determined to produce—or at least bread that resembles it—is everywhere. But then I'd try to give it to a couple of ladies from the neighborhood, and they'd carry on; "It's so dark! Aren't you going to learn to make lighter bread?"

"Nope," I'd say defiantly. "I'm not going to, so just try it my way and come back and tell me what you think."

I sounded confident, but hovering over me was a cloud of doubt. Was this thing real? Was I making something that was actually good? I can't tell you how indebted I am to the few people who for one reason or another took notice early on. A lot of the initial attention was a demonstration of the Joe Allen press operation at work (it was his money, after all): a notice in Liz Smith's column in the *Post* that he was opening a bakery, another in the *New York Times* with the headline "Joe Allen Bakes." But then there was the recognition from people who actually came to the bakery and ate the bread and met the baker. A brief piece in *New York* magazine described my basic loaf matter-of-factly, saying it "has a thick crust and a firm but airy crumb. It's about the size of a football and runs $2.75." (I sell it now, fifteen years later, for about a dollar more. I've never been as good a businessman as I should be.)

Then the wonderful Ed Levine, New York's bard of food observation, started to drop in, and he went on to tell my story briefly in his book *New York Eats*. Other attention began to come my way, so quickly it disoriented me at first. My style of baking was rapidly being accepted. Within a few years, Ruth Reichl in the *Times* described the bakery as "a church of bread." Things just kept looking up.

LESS IS MORE: NO-KNEAD BREAD

Sullivan Street breads were soon on restaurant tables across the city, and the bakery was gradually gaining a retail clientele. In fact, we needed to expand, and I opened a second Sullivan Street Bakery on West 47th Street in 2000. The original bakery is still there, owned by Joe Allen, but the name was changed to Grandaisy after I broke with my partner, Monica, who runs it now. My wife, Anitha (we'd met when she was an events planner in the restaurant industry, and we married in 2004), began encouraging me to put all my talk about the need for a culture of bread in this country, and my dreams of bringing bread baking to millions of home kitchens, into action by teaching baking classes. That would also, obviously, be a good marketing tool. As it turns out, teaching was immensely inspiring for me. It forced me to really streamline and explain my baking so that the new recipes I was developing could be used easily at home. And in doing so, I began working on developing my no-knead technique. I knew that if bread had been baked far and wide throughout history, from India to Scotland, it couldn't have been the daunting task it later became. It must have been easy.

It won't surprise you to hear that I looked to Italy, and specifically to ancient Rome, more often than to the modern baking books that lined my shelves. When I set out to create the simplest, most basic bread recipe for my classes, I went into my library and reached for the writings of Apicius, the great Roman cookbook writer. It didn't seem likely to me that ancient Roman bakers did any kneading at all. I figured they just shaped the risen fermented dough and baked it. Inspired by this realization, I began to reduce the amount of kneading in my recipes, and I started to see an interesting relationship between kneading and fermentation. When I worked the dough less but let it rise longer, it seemed to develop a structure as strong as, if not stronger than, what I had been getting from a longer kneading and shorter rising time. And to replicate a cloche, an ancient ceramic baking vessel, I simply preheated a Dutch oven, then dropped in a round of dough.

In 2004, the Tuscan chef Cesare Casella was booked to put on a special dinner at the James Beard Foundation in Greenwich Village. He liked the classic Italian breads I was producing at Sullivan Street and knew something about my interests, so he asked me to bake bread for this dinner, in the style of ancient Rome. For this occasion, I was going to reach further into the past than I ever had before. Driven by the idea of creating something ancient, primitive, and essential, I started from scratch, leaving tradition behind and simply doing what made sense to me. Using half whole wheat (which helped echo the wheat of ancient Rome, which was less refined than it generally is today) and half spelt, an early strain of wheat that still exists, I made roundish loaves and scored them as they appeared in pictures I'd seen of the carbonized bread excavated at Pompeii. And, as in my classes, I didn't do any kneading. The bread was terrific. It was denser than the loaf I'd make with today's bread flour, a bit gritty. Sure, it was showmanship, but it felt authentic.

As for the no-knead aspect of baking, I was completely sold on it. My technique was by now fully evolved (although I'm always tinkering). Applied in the modern home kitchen, it requires about 5 minutes of actual labor, followed by 12 to 18 hours in which the bread rises, developing structure and flavor on autopilot, and then another short rising time, and, finally, the brief baking in a covered pot. It's a terrific loaf of bread, easily within the reach of any home cook.

CHAPTER 2

The Lahey Method for No-Knead Bread in a Pot

The great chestnut-colored, chewy, satisfying loaf of bread that you're going to produce using the recipe in this chapter is nothing short of miraculous. Just think. It starts out with four completely ordinary ingredients: water (of which almost the entirety of the world and all of our bodies consists), flour (a milled grain), and a bit of salt and yeast. By the end of the process, those ingredients will have been transformed into the staff of life. Bread is part of who we are as human beings, and baking is a practice that, like hunting and fishing, predates recorded history.

The Miracle—How It Happens

FLOUR, WATER, AND TIME

How does this ancient miracle occur? Mixing flour and water together allows the gluten molecules in the flour to organize themselves into strands of sinew, the "muscles" of the dough that keep it strong as it inflates. Convention has it that extensive mixing and kneading will create a strongly structured dough relatively quickly. But that labor, I've discovered, isn't necessary. Learn to take it easy. Often the overly labor-intensive approach results in bread that looks okay but is tougher, more resistant when you bite into it. This same sad loaf is generally less flavorful (because of the shortened fermentation period that usually follows lengthy mixing and kneading) than if you had allowed the dough to do the job itself.

At the mixing stage, my only objective is to thoroughly combine the flour, water, yeast, and salt—nothing more. It's the unusually long first rise that does the job we have come to expect bakers to accomplish through kneading. I simply place the quickly mixed dough in a container to ferment overnight, where it slowly expands, ultimately developing the bubbling, slightly darkened look that demonstrates that the yeast is at work. When it's fully fermented, it forms those long strands of gluten that you'll see as you pull the dough out of the bowl. This slow, gentle process results, in my view, in the best and most traditional, flavorful loaf—a superior product to anything that can be produced by a bakery.

Harold McGee, author of *On Food and Cooking* (a revolutionary book that turned him into an almost legendary spokesman for the scientific understanding of cooking), explained how my no-knead method worked to Mark Bittman when Bittman first wrote about my technique for his *Minimalist* column in the *New York Times*. Quoted in the article, McGee summed up the mechanics of the transformation that I had discovered intuitively. "The long, slow rise brings the gluten molecules into side-by-side alignment to maximize their opportunity to bind to each other and produce a strong, elastic network. The wetness of the dough is an important piece of this because the gluten molecules are more mobile when there is a sufficient quantity of water, and so can move into alignment easier and faster than if the dough were stiff."

Something else happens when water and flour are mixed: enzymes present in the flour are activated and assist in breaking it down into sugars. The enzymes make the starch in the flour more easily digestible by the yeast (the sugars also contribute to the sweet wheaten taste of the finished product).

YEAST AND SALT

The ingredient that turns flour and water into risen bread is yeast. A primitive single-celled fungus, commercial yeast is dormant when dry, but when it meets water, it wakes up hungry. (In this book, I'm not going to burden you with the time and effort involved in cultivating natural yeast.) In the mix of flour and water, the yeast begins metabolizing the available sugars, converting them into carbon dioxide and alcohol as its cells rapidly multiply. This is fermentation—the same process that turns sugary grape juice into complex-tasting wine. During fermentation, the alcohol produced by the yeast contributes a pleasantly acrid character to the bread (the alcohol itself later burns off in the oven).

The long fermentation I propose means that only a tiny amount of yeast is required, since it will have plenty of time to grow and do its job, and I've found that in such small quantities, it doesn't matter much whether you use instant or another type of active dry yeast. A benefit to using a smaller amount of yeast is that it makes room for naturally occurring flavorful bacteria that are attracted to flour to enter into the equation during the 12- to 18-hour fermentation. These bacteria attack proteins, which they metabolize into compounds that contribute to the acidic, complex flavors of a well-fermented bread dough. At the bakery, I often test the pH, a measure of acidity, in my fermented bread dough. The acidity level is a consistent indicator of whether or not the dough is fully fermented. A pH level of 7 is neutral, so anything below that is acidic to some degree; a pH of 5.2 is pretty much perfect for my basic dough. If you want to try this yourself, you can find pH indicators sold all over the Internet (usually for testing the water in swimming pools or aquariums); a basic one should run between $60 and $70. But you can certainly get away without one.

You'll get to know the other telltale signs of perfect acidity, such as a bubbly surface that appears darkened and a dough that has a sour, tangy aroma. Using a minimal amount of yeast also encourages the flavor of the wheat itself to come through—as opposed to being overwhelmed by that yeasty flavor you probably recognize from simple, quicker bread recipes.

The carbon dioxide bubbles produced by the feeding yeast are responsible for the rising of bread dough. In a sufficiently developed dough, as fermentation takes place, the gluten structure traps this gas, thus accomplishing the inflation trick. An undeveloped gluten structure would allow those bubbles to escape, and you'd end up with a cracker. As for the bit of salt in the mixture, it adds flavor, of course, but it also slightly inhibits the activity of the yeast by making it harder for the yeast to get to the sugars resulting from the breakdown of the flour—and this ensures that the yeast won't force the dough to expand so quickly that the gluten bonds are broken. Again, limiting the action of the yeast leaves room for some flavor-giving bacterial action.

HEAT

When you put a loaf into the oven, the first blast of heat to hit the still-fermenting dough causes the most intense fermentation of all, in what is called "oven spring." The yeast goes crazy. The trapped gases emanating from the frantic yeast rapidly expand the dough, and then, abruptly, in just a few minutes, the dough reaches about 140 degrees Fahrenheit and the yeast dies, its work done. Inside, the interior firms as the moisture evaporates. As the interior of the loaf steams and cooks, the exterior colors and takes on a flavor of its own. The intense heat at the surface of the dough caramelizes the proteins and sugars (a process called the Maillard reaction, which is also exactly what happens when you char a steak), creating the savory, complex flavors of all well-browned foods, from French fries to toast to caramel sauce.

It is as if you were creating two separate objects simultaneously, that moist interior and the crunchy exterior. Steam from the moist dough helps keep the crust supple and prevents it from burning, allowing the interior to cook through before the crust hardens. Without sufficient steam, the crust would quickly become a brittle shell, preventing expansion and insulating the interior from the heat.

After the baked bread is removed from the oven, there's a final step in the process. All that romanticism about how delicious a loaf tastes fresh out of the oven is foolishness: the cooling step is crucial. Thorough cooling actually completes the cooking of the dough, and when you slice a hot loaf, you are releasing heat and moisture prematurely. The bread will taste underbaked and wet. Cooling may take just a few minutes or more than an hour, depending on the size of the loaf. The key is to wait until the bread has stopped "singing"—that crackling sound as steam escapes (see page 47) and feels only slightly warm to the touch. Then have at it!

In the basic recipes here, I specify 475 degrees Fahrenheit as the oven temperature, since this works for most people. But you might test out a range of temperatures, from 450 to 500 degrees Fahrenheit, because ovens vary. Many of the people who have baked the bread often have found their own ideal temperature through trial and error (though they may well have achieved excellent results throughout the range). If you have a noticeably hot or cool oven, adjust the temperature by 25 degrees one way or the other.

AN OVEN WITHIN AN OVEN—THE POT

In addition to a medium (3-quart) mixing bowl, a set of volume measures (cups and spoons) or a kitchen scale (my preference: see "Weighing Your Options," page 48), and a sturdy wooden spoon or rubber spatula or bowl scraper, there is only one essential piece of equipment needed for my basic recipe: the enclosure, the oven within the oven, the pot. It accomplishes what classic domed brick ovens do: it completely seals in the baking process so the steam escaping from the bread can do its work to ensure a good crust and a moist crumb.

I've seen a lot of recipes designed to approximate the steam-injected high-heat ovens that many professional bakers use. They involve tricks like throwing ice cubes onto the hot floor of the oven, misting the oven walls with a spray bottle, or preheating a cast-iron pan and then pouring in boiling water when you're ready to bake. And there has been plenty written about the use of pizza stones or ceramic tiles to better hold heat, the idea

Bread equipment: **1** scale; **2** measuring cups; **3** dough cutter; **4** measuring spoons; **5** chef's knife; **6** wooden spoon; **7** rubber spatula.

Bread equipment: **1** bowls; **2** rack; **3** baking sheet; **4** tea towel; **5** measuring cup; **6** brushes; **7** timer.

being that they create a mini brick oven within your oven. But I've found that baking in a preheated, covered heavy pot (one you probably already own) is a simple way to seal in the steam the wet dough releases and embrace the loaf in intense, intimate heat.

I developed most of my recipes for baking in a 4½- to 5½-quart pot. I often use an enameled cast-iron Le Creuset. Many who've used this brand have reported on various Web sites that the handle can burn in the oven, and in fact the company considers them ovenproof only up to 375 degrees Fahrenheit. (Not long after my basic recipe was published, a spate of petty thefts at cookware stores involved these handles, presumably to replace the ruined ones.) If you'd prefer to keep the one you've got, do what I did: Use a regular screwdriver or a butter knife to unscrew the handle and remove it. Then either put the screw back in to seal the hole (it will dangle, with nothing to catch on, so you need to be sure you don't lift the lid sideways and let it fall out) or fill the hole with a plug of aluminum foil. Much cheaper than Le Creuset, and every bit as effective, is the classic 5-quart Lodge preseasoned cast-iron pot. It's sold just about everywhere—cookware shops, hardware stores. I confess, though, that my favorite pot is probably the most expensive option, the all-ceramic Emile Henry. The high-quality ceramic, like iron, transmits heat evenly and well, but it's lighter than cast iron. In the end, they'll all do the job, by which I mean there's no discernible difference in flavor.

SINGING

Just after you take a loaf out of the oven, something strange often happens: it begins to make weird noises, a rapid-fire cracking sound, one pop after another. This "singing," as some bakers call it, is especially loud and obvious in the professional bakery, where dozens of loaves may be pulled out of an oven at the same time and placed together in a basket. They become a kind of snapping chorus. The singing lasts for several minutes—the temperature in the room will determine how long—as the bread cools.

This singing is evidence of the last phase of cooking, which takes place out of the oven—and it is why you should always give a loaf time to cool before slicing into it. The exterior of the loaf is very dry at the moment it's removed, but the interior is still wet. During cooling, the two elements of the bread start to even out somewhat, although the crust will remain brittle and the crumb soft. The crust is shrinking and cracking. Steam escapes through the cracks, which is the racket you hear, as it forces its way through, while the crumb solidifies. At this moment, the bread seems alive. I know that's a romantic idea, but it's how you get to feel when you fall in love with a simple, but beautifully baked rustic loaf.

WEIGHING YOUR OPTIONS

Plenty, probably most, home cooks in America do their baking without the use of a kitchen scale, but measuring by weight is the norm in many other parts of the world, and certainly in professional bakeries. Weight measurements are crucial for precisely standardized results. When you measure only by volume, there is a lot of room for variance: a cup of flour can differ in amount, depending on how densely it's packed, but the weight will be accurate no matter what. So I've included the metric weights in this book for those who want to use them at home. If you don't have a scale but plan to make a lot of bread, I urge you to get one: a balance type, a small spring scale, or a battery-operated digital scale—any of these will do. There are many brands, and I don't want to endorse one; generally they cost less than $40. Still, if you don't want to bother, go ahead and bake anyway. These recipes, as I will remind you often, are very forgiving.

A NOTE ON BREAD FLOUR

While I have made successful loaves of my basic bread using all-purpose flour, I call for bread flour in this book. Bread flour is usually milled from what is known as hard red "spring wheat" (sown in the spring, harvested in the fall), as opposed to softer "winter wheat" (planted in winter, harvested in the spring), which contains fewer of the proteins that, together with water, create gluten. The protein content of flour determines how much water it can absorb and the capacity it has to develop gluten and expand into a well-aerated, chewy loaf.

Most bread flour contains 13 to 14 grams of protein per cup. I've found that my recipes work well with any flour containing at least 11.5 grams of protein per cup. But all-purpose flour varies from brand to brand (the package won't give you a clue), and even regionally across America. Some all-purpose flours sold in the South—land of fluffy cakes and tender biscuits—can contain as little as 9 grams of protein per cup. Bread flour offers more consistent results.

STORING BREAD

I like to use my bread quickly, within 2 or 3 days, and I find the best way to keep it for that short period is wrapped in wax or butcher paper or in a paper bag at room temperature. Once it dries beyond the point where it's pleasant to eat, I try to make some other use of it (see Chapter Six, Stale Bread). Plastic wrap is a bad option; it toughens bread, makes it rubbery, and increases the likelihood of mold. And I'm no fan of refrigeration, which, among other things, usually imparts the tastes and odors of the refrigerator to a loaf. It also creates moisture, making it more likely that mold will form.

The Basic No-Knead Bread Recipe

Here's my basic no-knead, long-fermented rustic bread, a round loaf, or *boule*. It's an adaptation for the home kitchen of the much larger oval *filone* and the football-shaped *pugliese* sold at the Sullivan Street Bakery. I suggest you try this before any of the variations in Chapter Three, to get the hang of it. Even if you've baked before, the process is probably nothing like what your experience would lead you to expect. For one thing, many people who bake this bread find the dough to be unusually wet. Remember that most of the water is meant to be released as steam in the covered pot, and you'll be handling the dough very little anyway.

Don't feel too uptight about any of this. For example, I specify that the dough should rise at room temperature, about 72 degrees Fahrenheit. (In many of the recipes, I say to put the dough in a warm, draft-free spot—same thing.) But if that's not what you have at the moment, you'll be okay anyway. Just pay attention to the visual cues: At the end of the first rise, the dough is properly fermented when it has developed a darkened appearance and bubbles, and long, thread-like strands cling to the bowl when it's moved. After the second, briefer, rise, the loaf has risen sufficiently if it holds the impression of your fingertip when you poke it lightly, making an indentation about ¼ inch deep. It should hold that impression. If it springs back, let it rise for another 15 minutes.

Despite my own efforts to get this and all the other recipes in this book to reflect what I think is the optimal approach, conditions are going to vary from kitchen to kitchen. I hope you'll ultimately have the confidence to experiment yourself, adjusting the ingredients and timing to your own taste and circumstances. As the journalists who've reported on my bread have written, even the loaves that aren't what you'd regard as perfect are way better than fine.

ON TIMING: This bread is incredibly simple and involves little labor, but you need to plan ahead. Although mixing takes almost no time, the first rise requires from 12 to 18 hours. Then you'll need to shape the dough and let it rise for another 1 to 2 hours. The longer rise tends to result in a richer bread, but you need the patience and the schedule to do it. In any event, the shorter rise is acceptable too: Just pay attention to the signs of a good rise described in the recipes. A reminder: The visual cues—a bubbly surface with a darkened appearance—are key. Usually, 18 hours is optimal. (**Very cold weather exception:** In the dead of winter, when the dough will tend to rise more slowly, a longer period may be necessary, as much as 24 hours.)

After preheating the oven and the pot, you've got 30 minutes of covered baking, another 15 to 30 of uncovered baking, and about an hour of cooling. And, please, don't gulp down that first slice. Think of the first bite as you would the first taste of a glass of wine: smell it (there should be that touch of maltiness), chew it slowly to appreciate its almost meaty texture, and sense where it came from in its hint of wheat. Enjoy it. You baked it, and you did a good job.

YIELD: One 10-inch round loaf; 1¼ pounds
EQUIPMENT: A 4½- to 5½-quart heavy pot

INGREDIENTS	MEASURE	WEIGHT
bread flour	3 cups	400 grams
table salt	1¼ teaspoons	8 grams
instant or other active dry yeast	¼ teaspoon	1 gram
cool (55 to 65 degrees F) water	1⅓ cups	300 grams
wheat bran, cornmeal, or additional flour for dusting		

1. In a medium bowl, stir together the flour, salt, and yeast. Add the water and, using a wooden spoon or your hand, mix until you have a wet, sticky dough, about 30 seconds. Make sure it's really sticky to the touch; if it's not, mix in another tablespoon or two of water. Cover the bowl with a plate, tea towel, or plastic wrap and let sit at room temperature (about 72 degrees F), out of direct sunlight, until the surface is dotted with bubbles and the dough is more than doubled in size. This will take a minimum of 12 hours and (my preference) up to 18 hours. This slow rise—fermentation—is the key to flavor.

2. When the first fermentation is complete, generously dust a work surface (a wooden or plastic cutting board is fine) with flour. Use a bowl scraper or rubber spatula to scrape the dough onto the board in one piece. When you begin to pull the dough away from the bowl, it will cling in long, thin strands (this is the developed gluten), and it will be quite

loose and sticky—do not add more flour. Use lightly floured hands or a bowl scraper or spatula to lift the edges of the dough in toward the center. Nudge and tuck in the edges of the dough to make it round.

3. Place a cotton or linen tea towel (not terry cloth, which tends to stick and may leave lint in the dough) or a large cloth napkin on your work surface and generously dust the cloth with wheat bran, cornmeal, or flour. Use your hands or a bowl scraper or wooden spatula to gently lift the dough onto the towel, so it is seam side down. If the dough is tacky, dust the top lightly with wheat bran, cornmeal, or flour. Fold the ends of the towel loosely over the dough to cover it and place it in a warm, draft-free spot to rise for 1 to 2 hours. The dough is ready when it is almost doubled. If you gently poke it with your finger, making an indentation about ¼ inch deep, it should hold the impression. If it doesn't, let it rise for another 15 minutes.

4. Half an hour before the end of the second rise, preheat the oven to 475 degrees F, with a rack in the lower third position, and place a covered 4½- to 5½-quart heavy pot in the center of the rack.

5. Using pot holders, carefully remove the preheated pot from the oven and uncover it. Unfold the tea towel, lightly dust the dough with flour or bran, lift up the dough, either on the towel or in your hand, and quickly but gently invert it into the pot, seam side up. (Use caution—the pot will be very hot; see photos, page 55.) Cover the pot and bake for 30 minutes.

6. Remove the lid and continue baking until the bread is a deep chestnut color but not burnt, 15 to 30 minutes more. Use a heatproof spatula or pot holders to carefully lift the bread out of the pot and place it on a rack to cool thoroughly. Don't slice or tear into it until it has cooled, which usually takes at least an hour.

The Basic No-Knead Bread Recipe in Pictures

1 Mixing flour, salt, and yeast. 2 Adding the water. 3 Stirring to get a wet, sticky dough. 4 The dough. 5 Taking off the plastic wrap after the dough has doubled. 6 The fully fermented dough. 7 Using a bowl scraper to remove the dough in one piece. 8 Scraping the fermented dough onto a floured surface.

CONTINUES ON NEXT PAGE

9 Starting to fold the dough. **10** & **11** Folding and shaping the dough for the second rise. **12** Placing the dough onto a tea towel dusted with bran. **13** Dusting the dough with bran. **14** Folding the towel over the dough. **15** Unwrapping the dough after the second rise. **16** Dusting the dough before putting it in the pot. **17** The heated pot.

18 Positioning the dough for the pot. **19** Inverting the dough into the pot. **20** The loaf ready to be baked. **21** Baked loaf after uncovering the pot. **22** Using a wooden spatula to take bread out of the hot pot. **23** The bread cooling on a rack. **24** Bread after cooling and slicing.

Stecca (page 77).

CHAPTER 3

Specialties of the House

Although many of the recipes you will find in this book closely resemble my basic no-knead bread (see page 50), when I vary the ingredients list with the likes of walnuts, olives, or cheese, it sometimes leads to slight differences in how a loaf is prepared. The adjustments reflect my own preferences: a bit less salt in one, a bit of pepper in another. Olives will add both salt and liquid to the basic dough, to take one example. Feel free, once you've done it my way, to adjust the recipe if, say, you'd like a touch more salt or want your bread darker or lighter. This book is all about learning to bake with the Lahey approach, not robotically following instructions.

Also, although the breads in this chapter are derived from the loaves sold at Sullivan Street, the results will not, of course, be identical to the bakery's breads. For one thing, without our professional ovens, you're not going to be able to make loaves as large as I do in the bakery. So the huge *filones* and the football-shaped *pugliese* I mentioned earlier are not here in the form you'd find them in my bakery; rather, these are simply oval versions of the basic recipe for the round loaf in the previous chapter. Even so, I swear some of the bread you will bake at home will be just as satisfying as if you'd bought it at the bakery—or maybe even better, suited to your own tastes as you customize the recipes and feel that rush of accomplishment.

GENERAL EQUIPMENT NOTE: Most of the bread recipes require the covered 4½- to 5½-quart enameled or cast-iron pot I describe on page 45. Again, I urge you to use a kitchen scale rather than volume measures, because a scale is more precise. Of course you'll also need the most common tools, like bowls, a bowl scraper or a rubber spatula, a wooden spoon, and a rack for cooling. When other more specialized equipment is called for (an extraction juicer, for instance), the recipe will list it at the outset.

A NOTE ON INSTRUCTIONS: I hope you followed my advice in the previous chapter and baked the basic bread there before moving on to these loaves. The instructions are more detailed there than here, because I assume you need less expansive guidance now. That said, I haven't left anything to chance in these recipes, just pared them down a bit, but if you need more details, review the basic recipe on page 50.

Pane Integrale.

Pane Integrale • WHOLE WHEAT BREAD

White flour is made from the bulk of the wheat kernel, the starchy endosperm. Whole wheat flour takes more from the plant. In addition to the endosperm, it retains the bran, which is the fibrous outer husk of the kernel, and the germ, which contains the oil in the grain. Make no mistake: the endosperm of a wheat kernel is nourishing all by itself. But incorporating the bran and germ results in a more fiber- and nutrient-rich food. So I played around a bit with my basic formula.

First I applied my technique to 100-percent whole wheat bread, and while it made good toast, I found that it was too gritty, too dense for my taste. Whole wheat lacks some of the elasticity of white bread flours. So I kept cutting down the ratio until I got to around 25-percent whole wheat flour—and finally I was content. (Actually, before milling was as efficient as it is now, there was always a significant portion of the bran left behind in white flour, so this ratio more closely resembles preindustrial bread.)

I invite you to try the experiment yourself if you're interested in finding your own favorite ratio. Go all the way with 100-percent whole wheat flour, then drop down to 85 or 50 percent, or lower. If you've got health reasons to get a lot of fiber into your diet, a high proportion of whole wheat might do the trick; so might adding other grains like flaxseed. And maybe you'll actually prefer the taste and feel of bread based on a higher ratio of whole wheat than the one I offer here.

YIELD: One 10-inch round loaf; 1¼ pounds
EQUIPMENT: A 4½- to 5½-quart heavy pot

INGREDIENTS	MEASURE	WEIGHT
bread flour	2¼ cups	300 grams
whole wheat flour	¾ cup	100 grams
table salt	1¼ teaspoons	8 grams
instant or other active dry yeast	½ teaspoon	2 grams
cool (55 to 65 degrees F) water	1⅓ cups	300 grams
wheat bran, cornmeal, or additional flour for dusting		

RECIPE CONTINUES ON NEXT PAGE

1. In a medium bowl, stir together the flours, salt, and yeast. Add the water and, using a wooden spoon or your hand, mix until you have a wet, sticky dough, about 30 seconds. Cover the bowl and let sit at room temperature until the surface is dotted with bubbles and the dough is more than doubled in size, 12 to 18 hours.

2. When the first rise is complete, generously dust a work surface with flour. Use a bowl scraper or rubber spatula to scrape the dough out of the bowl in one piece. Using lightly floured hands or a bowl scraper or spatula, lift the edges of the dough in toward the center. Nudge and tuck in the edges of the dough to make it round.

3. Place a tea towel on your work surface and generously dust it with wheat bran, cornmeal, or flour. Gently place the dough on the towel, seam side down. If the dough is tacky, dust the top lightly with wheat bran, cornmeal, or flour. Fold the ends of the tea towel loosely over the dough to cover it and place it in a warm, draft-free spot to rise for 1 to 2 hours. The dough is ready when it is almost doubled. If you gently poke it with your finger, it should hold the impression. If it springs back, let it rise for another 15 minutes.

4. Half an hour before the end of the second rise, preheat the oven to 475 degrees F, with a rack positioned in the lower third, and place a covered 4½- to 5½-quart heavy pot in the center of the rack.

5. Using pot holders, carefully remove the preheated pot from the oven and uncover it. Unfold the tea towel and quickly but gently invert the dough into the pot, seam side up. (Use caution—the pot will be very hot; see photos, page 55.) Cover the pot and bake for 30 minutes.

6. Remove the lid and continue baking until the bread is a deep chestnut color but not burnt, 15 to 30 minutes more. Use a heatproof spatula or pot holders to carefully lift the bread out of the pot and place it on a rack to cool thoroughly.

Rye Bread

The most notable Italian rye bread is from Bolzano in northeastern Italy, an area that was once Austrian, and it's a bread that might just as easily be Middle European as Italian. Rye thrives better in the northern cold climate than wheat does. Rye flour always has to be combined with some wheat flour, because rye just doesn't have the necessary gluten to expand properly, but the flavor is nevertheless distinctive and satisfying. It's a bit tangy, like sourdough, and the loaf has a handsome dark interior.

YIELD: One 10-inch round loaf; 1¼ pounds
EQUIPMENT: A 4½- to 5½-quart heavy pot

INGREDIENTS	MEASURE	WEIGHT
bread flour	2¼ cups	300 grams
rye flour	¾ cup	100 grams
table salt	1¼ teaspoons	8 grams
instant or other active dry yeast	½ teaspoon	2 grams
cool (55 to 65 degrees F) water	1⅓ cups	300 grams
rye flour for dusting		

1. In a medium bowl, stir together the flours, salt, and yeast. Add the water and, using a wooden spoon or your hand, mix until you have a wet, sticky dough, about 30 seconds. Cover the bowl and let sit at room temperature until the surface is dotted with bubbles and the dough is more than doubled in size, 12 to 18 hours.

2. When the first rise is complete, generously dust a work surface with flour. Use a bowl scraper or rubber spatula to scrape the dough out of the bowl in one piece. Using lightly floured hands or a bowl scraper or spatula, lift the edges of the dough in toward the center. Nudge and tuck in the edges of the dough to make it round.

RECIPE CONTINUES ON NEXT PAGE

3. Place a tea towel on your work surface and generously dust it with rye flour. Gently place the dough on the towel, seam side down. If the dough is tacky, dust the top lightly with rye flour. Fold the ends of the tea towel loosely over the dough to cover it and place it in a warm, draft-free spot to rise for 1 to 2 hours. The dough is ready when it is almost doubled. If you gently poke it with your finger, it should hold the impression. If it springs back, let it rise for another 15 minutes.

4. Half an hour before the end of the second rise, preheat the oven to 475 degrees F, with a rack in the lower third, and place a covered 4½- to 5½-quart heavy pot in the center of the rack.

5. Using pot holders, carefully remove the preheated pot from the oven and uncover it. Unfold the tea towel and quickly but gently invert the dough into the pot, seam side up. (Use caution—the pot will be very hot; see photos, page 55.) Cover the pot and bake for 30 minutes.

6. Remove the lid and continue baking until the bread is a deep chestnut color but not burnt, 15 to 30 minutes more. Use a heatproof spatula or pot holders to carefully lift the bread out of the pot and place it on a rack to cool thoroughly.

Rye bread.

Pan co' Santi • WALNUT BREAD

When I was in Tuscany and my love affair with baking was growing, one of the most enjoyable yet simplest breads I learned about was a version of this raisin walnut bread. It's a classic, festive bread for the holidays, which I ate first on All Saints' Day (Tutti Santi Giorni).

YIELD: One 10-inch round loaf; 1½ pounds
EQUIPMENT: A 4½- to 5½-quart heavy pot

INGREDIENTS	MEASURE	WEIGHT
bread flour	3 cups	400 grams
raisins	½ cup	85 grams
chopped walnuts	½ cup	50 grams
table salt	1¼ teaspoons	8 grams
ground cinnamon	¾ teaspoon	2 grams
instant or other active dry yeast	½ teaspoon	2 grams
freshly ground black pepper	pinch	
cool (55 to 65 degrees F) water	1½ cups	350 grams
wheat bran, cornmeal, or additional flour for dusting		

1. In a medium bowl, stir together the flour, raisins, walnuts, salt, cinnamon, yeast, and pepper, mixing thoroughly. Add the water and, using a wooden spoon or your hand, mix until you have a wet, sticky dough, about 30 seconds. If it's not really sticky to the touch, mix in another tablespoon or two of water. Cover the bowl and let sit at room temperature until the surface is dotted with bubbles and the dough is more than doubled in size, 12 to 18 hours.

2. When the first rise is complete, generously dust a work surface with flour. Use a bowl scraper or rubber spatula to scrape the dough out of the bowl in one piece. Using lightly floured hands or a bowl scraper or spatula, lift the edges of the dough in toward the center. Nudge and tuck in the edges of the dough to make it round.

3. Place a tea towel on your work surface and generously dust it with wheat bran, cornmeal,

or flour. Gently place the dough on the towel, seam side down. If the dough is tacky, dust the top lightly with wheat bran, cornmeal, or flour. Fold the ends of the tea towel loosely over the dough to cover it and place it in a warm, draft-free spot to rise for 1 to 2 hours. The dough is ready when it is almost doubled. If you gently poke it with your finger, it should hold the impression. If it springs back, let it rise for another 15 minutes.

4. Half an hour before the end of the second rise, preheat the oven to 475 degrees F, with a rack in the lower third, and place the covered 4½- to 5½-quart heavy pot in the center of the rack.

5. Using pot holders, carefully remove the preheated pot from the oven and uncover it. Unfold the tea towel and quickly but gently invert the dough into the pot, seam side up. (Use caution—the pot will be very hot; see photos, page 55.) Cover the pot and bake for 30 minutes.

6. Remove the lid and continue baking until bread is a deep chestnut color but not burnt, 15 to 30 minutes more. Use a heatproof spatula or pot holders to gently lift the bread out of the pot and place it on a rack to cool thoroughly.

Pan co' Santi.

Pane all'Olive.

Pane all'Olive • OLIVE BREAD

When I first opened Sullivan Street, with Roman baking in mind, this slightly pungent olive loaf immediately became my signature bread. As a result of the brine the olives release during baking, this recipe calls for no salt.

YIELD: One 10-inch round loaf; 1½ pounds
EQUIPMENT: A 4½- to 5½-quart heavy pot

INGREDIENTS	MEASURE	WEIGHT
bread flour	3 cups	400 grams
roughly chopped pitted olives (see Note)	about 1½ cups	200 grams
instant or other active dry yeast	¾ teaspoon	3 grams
cool (55 to 65 degrees F) water	1½ cups	300 grams
wheat bran, cornmeal, or additional flour for dusting		

1. In a medium bowl, stir together the flour, olives, and yeast. Add the water and, using a wooden spoon or your hand, mix until you have a wet, sticky dough, about 30 seconds. Cover the bowl and let sit at room temperature until the surface is dotted with bubbles and the dough is more than doubled in size, 12 to 18 hours.

2. When the first rise is complete, generously dust a work surface with flour. Use a bowl scraper or rubber spatula to scrape the dough out of the bowl in one piece. Using lightly floured hands or a bowl scraper or spatula, lift the edges of the dough in toward the center. Nudge and tuck in the edges of the dough to make it round.

3. Place a tea towel on your work surface and generously dust it with wheat bran, cornmeal, or flour. Gently place the dough on the towel, seam side down. If the dough is tacky, dust the top lightly with wheat bran, cornmeal, or flour. Fold the ends of the tea towel loosely over the dough to cover it and place it in a warm, draft-free spot to rise for 1 to 2 hours.

RECIPE CONTINUES ON NEXT PAGE

The dough is ready when it is almost doubled. If you gently poke it with your finger, it should hold the impression. If it springs back, let it rise for another 15 minutes.

4. Half an hour before the end of the second rise, preheat the oven to 475 degrees F, with a rack in the lower third, and place a covered 4½- to 5½-quart heavy pot in the center of the rack.

5. Using pot holders, carefully remove the preheated pot from the oven and uncover it. Unfold the tea towel and quickly but gently invert the dough into the pot, seam side up. (Use caution—the pot will be very hot; see photos, page 55.) Cover the pot and bake for 30 minutes.

6. Remove the lid and continue baking until the bread is a deep chestnut color but not burnt, 15 to 30 minutes more. Use a heatproof spatula or pot holders to gently lift the bread out of the pot and place it on a rack to cool thoroughly.

NOTE: For this loaf, any pitted olive will yield something worth eating. (You don't want to go to the trouble of pitting them yourself, because it is tedious and the results will not be as neat.) But what I turn to most often are pitted kalamata olives soaked in a pure salt brine—nothing else, just salt. A commonly available kalamata that I'm very fond of is made by Divina and can be found at many supermarkets and gourmet stores. You might think that because they're black they will change the color of the bread, but they won't, unless you carelessly dump some of the brine into the dough. Green Sicilian colossals, sometimes called "giant" olives, packed in pure salt brine, are another good option; they're often available at Italian food stores.

Pane con Formaggio • CHEESE BREAD

Cheese and bread, both products of controlled fermentation, are natural, ancient partners—you find them complementing each other in much of the world. The inspiration for this particular bread is a traditional Easter loaf of cheese-laden brioche that I ate in Rome. I've adapted the idea to my no-knead, long-fermentation approach, suffusing my standard bread dough (rather than using an egg-rich brioche dough) with intensely cheesy flavor. For this recipe, I like to use pecorino Toscano. I must have had this sheep's-milk cheese nearly every day I spent in Tuscany, and its flavor, mild but with a characteristic slight bite, is filled with happy memories for me of my time in Italy. I recommend seeking out a pecorino that's been aged for only three months so it's still mild and semisoft.

YIELD: One 10-inch round loaf; 1½ pounds
EQUIPMENT: A 4½- to 5½-quart heavy pot

INGREDIENTS	MEASURE	WEIGHT
bread flour	3 cups	400 grams
pecorino Toscano, Asiago, or aged Fontina, cut into ½-inch cubes (see Note)	about 2½ cups	200 grams
table salt (see Note)	1 teaspoon	6 grams
instant or other active dry yeast	¾ teaspoon	3 grams
freshly ground black pepper	½ teaspoon	2 grams
cool (55 to 65 degrees F) water	1⅓ cups	300 grams
wheat bran, cornmeal, or additional flour for dusting		

1. In a medium bowl, stir together the flour, cheese, salt, yeast, and pepper. Add the water and, using a wooden spoon or your hand, mix until you have a wet, sticky dough, about 30 seconds. Cover the bowl and let sit at room temperature until the surface is dotted with bubbles and the dough is more than doubled in size, 12 to 18 hours.

2. When the first rise is complete, generously dust a work surface with flour. Use a bowl scraper or rubber spatula to scrape the dough out of the bowl in one piece. Using lightly

RECIPE CONTINUES ON NEXT PAGE

floured hands or a bowl scraper or spatula, lift the edges of the dough in toward the center. Nudge and tuck in the edges of the dough to make it round.

3. Place a tea towel on your work surface and generously dust it with wheat bran, cornmeal, or flour. Gently place the dough on the towel, seam side down. If the dough is tacky, dust the top lightly with wheat bran, cornmeal, or flour. Fold the ends of the tea towel loosely over the dough to cover it and place it in a warm, draft-free spot to rise for 1 to 2 hours. The dough is ready when it is almost doubled. If you gently poke it with your finger, it should hold the impression. If it springs back, let it rise for another 15 minutes.

4. Half an hour before the end of the second rise, preheat the oven to 475 degrees F, with a rack in the lower third, and place a covered 4½- to 5½-quart heavy pot in the center of the rack.

5. Using pot holders, carefully remove the preheated pot from the oven and uncover it. Unfold the tea towel and quickly but gently invert the dough into the pot, seam side up. (Use caution—the pot will be very hot; see photos, page 55.) Cover the pot and bake for 30 minutes.

Pane con Formaggio.

6. Remove the lid and continue baking until the bread is a deep chestnut color but not burnt, 15 to 30 minutes more. Use a heatproof spatula or pot holders to gently lift the bread out of the pot and place it on a rack to cool thoroughly.

NOTE: Taste the cheese you buy: if it seems quite salty (which is likely if it's been aged for more than 3 months), reduce the salt in the recipe by half. Also, you don't have to use one of the cheeses I suggest—this bread is a great place to showcase any of your favorite firm or semifirm cheeses.

Pancetta Bread

Old-time Italian bakers hate to waste anything. One way they use up bits of meat, like roast pork butt or sausage or leftover pancetta, is to work it into a loaf of bread. Invariably, when they make these breads, lard comes into the picture. The lard helps to make the dough more elastic, so it expands more than other loaves when it bakes. There used to be a bakery in SoHo, D&G, that was well known for its lard bread, and frequently the old guys around the neighborhood would ask me if I'd tried that lard bread yet. When I finally did, I loved it. This pancetta bread is my bow in that direction. I don't use additional fat, though, since it comes with the pancetta or bacon. And the pancetta (or bacon) isn't lost in there—you're aware of the meatiness of the loaf—so it's almost a sandwich in its own right.

YIELD: One 10-inch round loaf; 1½ pounds
EQUIPMENT: A 4½- to 5½-quart heavy pot

INGREDIENTS	MEASURE	WEIGHT
pancetta, sliced ¼-inch thick (by the deli) and cut into ¼-inch dice, or slab bacon, diced	about 2⅓ cups	300 grams
bread flour	3 cups	400 grams
table salt	½ teaspoon	3 grams
instant or other active dry yeast	¼ teaspoon	1 gram
hot red pepper flakes (optional)	¼ teaspoon or to taste	½ gram
cool (55 to 65 degrees F) water	1½ cups	350 grams
wheat bran, cornmeal, or additional flour for dusting		

1. Cook the pancetta or bacon in a heavy skillet over medium heat, stirring occasionally, until crisp and golden, about 10 minutes. Reserve 1 tablespoon of the fat. Drain the pancetta on paper towels and let cool.

2. In a medium bowl, stir together the flour, pancetta, salt, yeast, and red pepper flakes, if you're using them. Add the water and reserved rendered fat and, using a wooden spoon or your hand, mix until you have a wet, sticky dough, about 30 seconds. Cover the bowl

RECIPE CONTINUES ON NEXT PAGE

and let sit at room temperature until the surface is dotted with bubbles and the dough is more than doubled in size, 12 to 18 hours.

3. When the first rise is complete, generously dust a work surface with flour. Use a bowl scraper or rubber spatula to scrape the dough out of the bowl in one piece. Using lightly floured hands or a bowl scraper or spatula, lift the edges of the dough in toward the center. Nudge and tuck in the edges of the dough to make it round.

4. Place a tea towel on your work surface and generously dust it with wheat bran, cornmeal, or flour. Gently place the dough on the towel, seam side down. If the dough is tacky, dust the top lightly with wheat bran, cornmeal, or flour. Fold the ends of the tea towel loosely over the dough to cover it and place it in a warm, draft-free spot to rise for 1 to 2 hours. The dough is ready when it is almost doubled. If you gently poke it with your finger, it should hold the impression. If it springs back, let it rise for another 15 minutes.

5. Half an hour before the end of the second rise, preheat the oven to 475 degrees F, with a rack in the lower third, and place a covered 4½- to 5½-quart heavy pot in the center of the rack.

6. Using pot holders, carefully remove the preheated pot from the oven and uncover it. Unfold the tea towel and quickly but gently invert the dough into the pot, seam side up. (Use caution—the pot will be very hot; see photos, page 55.) Cover the pot and bake for 30 minutes.

7. Remove the lid and continue baking until the bread is a deep chestnut color but not burnt, 15 to 30 minutes more. Use a heatproof spatula or pot holders to carefully lift the bread out of the pot and place it on a rack to cool thoroughly.

VARIATION • PANCETTA ROLLS

For 20 pancetta rolls, double the recipe for pancetta bread and follow the directions through the second rise. Preheat the oven to 450 degrees F. Oil a baking pan. Transfer the dough onto a generously floured work surface. Cut the dough mound into four strips and break each strip into five equal pieces. Each piece should weigh about 80 grams. Round each piece into a roll-shaped ball. Place the balls on the pan in even rows. Bake for about 40 minutes, until the rolls are dark brown. Place them on a rack and allow them to cool thoroughly.

Pancetta Rolls in Pictures

1 Cutting the dough in half. **2** Cutting the dough into four equal strips. **3** Breaking the strips into five sections and shaping them. **4** Each ball ready to be placed on the oiled sheet. **5** The rolls after baking. **6** The rolls cooling on a rack.

Stecca in Pictures

1 Brushing the dough with olive oil. **2** Sprinkling the dough with salt. **3** After the second rise, dividing the dough. **4** Cutting the dough into quarters. **5** The strips before stretching. **6** Placing all four strips onto the baking sheet. **7** Pushing tomatoes, garlic, and olives into the dough for the stecca variation. **8** Brushing the stecca with olive oil. (See photo of finished stecca on page 56.)

Stecca • STICK OR SMALL BAGUETTE

The name of this bread—*stecca*, or "stick" in Italian—is one I simply made up to describe it, since it has a narrow shape. It's based on the faster-rising pizza bianca dough you'll find in the pizza section (see page 137) and is stretched into such a narrow rope that it bakes rapidly. It is also baked on a baking sheet rather than in a pot. In this case, even though I get a good, brittle crust, it's thinner than most of the other breads in this section. Because I wanted to use it for sandwiches (see Chapter Five), I was aiming for a lighter-colored, less-assertive loaf of bread to encase the filling ingredients without overpowering them. But the olive oil glaze and coarse salt make it very flavorful on its own.

YIELD: 4 thin stick-shaped 18-inch loaves; ⅓ pound each
EQUIPMENT: A 13-by-18-inch rimmed baking sheet

INGREDIENTS	MEASURE	WEIGHT
bread flour	3 cups	400 grams
table salt	½ teaspoon	3 grams
sugar	¾ teaspoon	3 grams
instant or other active dry yeast	¼ teaspoon	1 gram
cool (55 to 65 degrees F) water	1½ cups	350 grams
additional flour for dusting		
extra-virgin olive oil	¼ cup	about 60 grams
coarse sea salt	¾ teaspoon	3 grams

1. In a medium bowl, stir together the flour, table salt, sugar, and yeast. Add the water and, using a wooden spoon or your hand, mix until you have a wet, sticky dough, about 30 seconds. Cover the bowl and let sit at room temperature until the surface is dotted with bubbles and the dough is more than doubled in size, 12 to 18 hours.

2. When the first rise is complete, generously dust a work surface with flour. Use a bowl scraper or rubber spatula to scrape the dough out of the bowl in one piece. Fold the dough over itself two or three times and gently shape it into a somewhat flattened ball.

RECIPE CONTINUES ON NEXT PAGE

Brush the surface of the dough with some of the olive oil and sprinkle with ¼ teaspoon of the coarse salt (which will gradually dissolve on the surface).

3. Place a tea towel on your work surface and generously dust it with wheat bran, cornmeal, or flour. Gently place the dough on the towel, seam side down. If the dough is tacky, dust the top lightly with wheat bran, cornmeal, or flour. Fold the ends of the tea towel loosely over the dough to cover it and place in a warm, draft-free spot to rise for 1 to 2 hours. The dough is ready when it is almost doubled. If you gently poke it with your finger, it should hold the impression. If it springs back, let it rise for another 15 minutes.

4. Half an hour before the end of the second rise, preheat the oven to 500 degrees F, with a rack in the center. Oil a 13-by-18-by-1-inch baking sheet.

5. Cut the dough into quarters. Gently stretch each piece evenly into a stick shape approximately the length of the pan. Place on the pan, leaving at least 1 inch between the loaves. Brush with olive oil and sprinkle with the remaining ½ teaspoon coarse salt.

6. Bake for 15 to 25 minutes, until the crust is golden brown. Cool on the pan for 5 minutes, then use a spatula to transfer the stecca to a rack to cool thoroughly.

NOTE: The stecca may become a bit soggy in just a few hours because of the salt on the surface. If that happens, reheat the loaves in a hot oven until crisp.

VARIATION • STECCA POMODORI, ALL'OLIVE, O AL'AGLIO (STECCA WITH TOMATOES, OLIVES, OR GARLIC)

Push 10 cherry tomato halves, cut side up, 10 large pitted olives, or 10 lightly crushed garlic cloves into each formed stecca, taking care to space the additions evenly down the length of the dough. Brush each stecca with enough olive oil to create a thin coat of oil on the surface. For the tomato stecca, top each tomato half with a very thin slice of garlic and a couple of fresh thyme leaves, and sprinkle with salt. Sprinkle the garlic stecca with salt and freshly ground black pepper. Do not salt the olive stecca—it's already salty from the olives.

Stirato • ITALIAN BAGUETTE

This is the Italian version of the classic French baguette—its name means "stretched." This loaf isn't as long as we'd make it in the bakery, because home ovens wouldn't accommodate its size, and you don't have our special elongated pots to bake them in. (Unlike the Stecca, on page 77, I wanted to use the basic dough recipe and bake the bread in a pot for the more familiar pronounced crust.) For the home kitchen, I use a Römertopf French Bread Baker. The baker looks something like a terra-cotta flower planter. With my method, I turn the base upside down on a pizza stone. The baker becomes the lid, with the pizza stone (at least as large as the pot) as the base, creating that desirable bread-in-a-pot effect.

The instructions for the Römertopf tell you to soak the baker before baking in it and to place it in a cool oven, not a preheated one—the concern being that any abrupt change in temperature, hot or cold, might crack the clay. So my trick is to soak the pot and preheat it as you preheat the oven. When you remove the hot pizza stone and pot from the oven to add the dough, be sure not to put either piece down on a cold surface (I put a couple of towels out to protect them). (See frontispiece for photo of finished stirato.)

YIELD: Two 12-inch baguettes; ¾ pound each
EQUIPMENT: A pizza stone and a Römertopf French Bread Baker (see Note)

INGREDIENTS	MEASURE	WEIGHT
bread flour	3 cups	400 grams
table salt	1¼ teaspoons	8 grams
instant or other active dry yeast	¼ teaspoon	1 gram
cool (55 to 65 degrees F) water	1½ cups	300 grams
additional flour for dusting		

1. In a medium bowl, stir together the flour, salt, and yeast. Add the water and, using a wooden spoon or your hand, mix until you have a wet, sticky dough, about 30 seconds. Cover the bowl and let sit at room temperature until the surface is dotted with bubbles and the dough is more than doubled in size, 12 to 18 hours.

RECIPE CONTINUES ON NEXT PAGE

2. When the first rise is complete, generously dust a work surface with flour. Use a bowl scraper or rubber spatula to scrape the dough out of the bowl in one piece. Dust the surface of the dough with flour and nudge it into a rough rectangle about 8 by 10 inches. Lifting one long side of the rectangle with the thumb and index fingers of both hands, fold the dough over toward the center. Then gently roll the dough into a tube, using your fingers to help tuck the dough into the roll as you go. Cut it into 2 equal pieces.

3. Place the pieces of dough on a floured surface in a warm, draft-free spot and cover with a tea towel. Let rise until almost doubled in volume, about 30 minutes. If you gently poke the dough with your finger, it should hold the impression. If it springs back, let it rise for another 15 minutes.

4. Meanwhile, soak the clay bread baker for 10 minutes.

5. Half an hour before the end of the second rise, preheat the oven to 475 degrees F, with a rack in the center, and place the baker on the pizza stone, in the center of the rack.

6. Using pot holders, carefully remove the pot and stone from the oven, taking care not to set them on a cold surface. Dust the center of the stone with flour. Pick up 1 piece of dough (you will bake 1 loaf at a time) and flip it so the seam side is down. Holding the dough with both hands above the middle of the hot baking stone, gently and evenly stretch it into a flat loaf approximately 11 inches in length (not longer than the Römertopf pot), and place it on the stone. This stretching takes practice; at first your stirato may be a bit misshapen, but you'll get the hang of it. Using pot holders, cover the loaf with the inverted Römertopf pot, and bake for 20 minutes.

7. Uncover the loaf and place the pot on another rack in the oven, to keep it hot for the second loaf. Continue to bake the first stirato for 10 to 20 minutes, until the crust is light chestnut colored. Carefully remove the stone from the oven, using pot holders, and transfer the stirato to a rack to cool thoroughly. Shape and bake the second loaf in the same way.

NOTE: The Römertopf French Bread Baker is available in kitchenware stores and online; it has a 13-inch base and, at less than $30, is a terrific buy.

Ciabatta • SLIPPER LOAF

A ciabatta is not always slipper shaped—to quality for the name, Italian for "slipper," it just needs to be elongated, broad, and sort of flattish, which this is. This recipe is very similar to the one for stirato but is wider and flatter. To get that shape I used the familiar Römertopf Clay Baker instead of the French Bread Baker but dispensed with the lid and still used a pizza stone as the base.

YIELD: Two 10-by-5-inch loaves; ½ pound each
EQUIPMENT: A pizza stone and a Römertopf Clay Baker, 6- to 8-pound capacity (available in kitchenware stores and online)

INGREDIENTS	MEASURE	WEIGHT
bread flour	3 cups	400 grams
table salt	1¼ teaspoons	8 grams
instant or other active dry yeast	¼ teaspoon	1 gram
cool (55 to 65 degrees F) water	1½ cups	350 grams
additional flour for dusting		

1. In a medium bowl, stir together the flour, salt, and yeast. Add the water and, using a wooden spoon or your hand, mix until you have a wet, sticky dough, about 30 seconds. Cover the bowl and let sit at room temperature until the surface is dotted with bubbles and the dough is more than doubled in size, 12 to 18 hours.

2. When the first rise is complete, generously dust a work surface with flour. Use a bowl scraper or rubber spatula to scrape the dough out of the bowl in one piece. Dust the surface of the dough with flour and, with lightly floured hands, nudge the dough into roughly a 14-inch square. Fold the dough in half, and then crosswise in half again, so you have a square, roughly 7 inches on each side.

RECIPE CONTINUES ON NEXT PAGE

3. Place the dough in a warm, draft-free spot, cover it with a tea towel, and let rise for 1 hour. The dough is ready when it is almost doubled. If you gently poke it with your finger, it should hold the impression. If it springs back, let it rise for another 15 minutes.

4. Meanwhile, soak the clay baker for 10 minutes.

5. Half an hour before the end of the second rise, preheat the oven to 475 degrees F, with a rack in the center, place the baker on the pizza stone, and put them in the center of the rack.

6. Using pot holders, carefully remove the hot pot and stone from the oven, taking care not to set them on a cold surface. Using a dough cutter or sharp serrated knife, cut the dough in half. Shape each piece into a long flat loaf. Generously dust each loaf with flour (you will bake 1 loaf at a time). Pick up 1 loaf with both hands, quickly but gently stretch it to almost the length of the clay pot (roughly 10 inches), and place it on the stone. Using pot holders, cover the loaf with the inverted pot, and bake for 20 minutes.

7. Uncover the loaf and place the pot on another rack in the oven, to keep it hot for the second loaf. Continue to bake the first loaf for 10 to 20 minutes, checking the color of the loaf once or twice. It is done when the crust is a light chestnut color. Using pot holders, carefully remove the stone from the oven. Transfer the ciabatta to a rack to cool thoroughly, and bake the second ciabatta the same way.

Ciabatta
in Pictures

1 The Römertopf bread baker. **2** Cutting the dough. **3** Stretching the dough the length of the pot. **4** Covering the loaf with the inverted pot on the pizza stone. **5** Ciabatta after uncovering. **6** Finished loaf.

Coconut-Chocolate Bread.

Coconut-Chocolate Bread

When my bakery was still on Sullivan Street, there was a fabulous Jamaican spot nearby where I liked to buy jerk beef patties for lunch. One day the baker brought out a coconut bread. "The best in the world, mon, try it," he insisted. Soft, almost squishy, and sweet, it couldn't have been more different from my rustic Italian breads, but it was undeniably delicious. To gild the lily, the guy made sandwiches with this bread and spicy beef patties, creating one of those amazing counterpoints that linger in your taste memory forever. Inspired by that bread, and by my childhood passion for the coconut-chocolate combo in Mounds bars, I created this coconut-chocolate bread, using the basic technique.

YIELD: One 8-inch round loaf; 1½ pounds
EQUIPMENT: A 4½- to 5½-quart heavy pot

INGREDIENTS	MEASURE	WEIGHT
bread flour	2 cups plus 2 tablespoons	280 grams
unsweetened large-flake coconut	2 cups loosely packed	100 grams
semisweet chocolate chunks	1 cup	150 grams
table salt	¾ teaspoon	4 grams
instant or other active dry yeast	¼ teaspoon	1 gram
cool (55 to 65 degrees F) water	1¼ cups	280 grams
wheat bran or additional flour for dusting		

1. In a medium bowl, stir together the flour, half of the coconut, the chocolate, salt, and yeast. Add the water and, using a wooden spoon or your hands, mix until you have a wet, sticky dough, about 30 seconds. Cover the bowl and let sit at room temperature until the surface is puffy and the dough is more than doubled in size, 12 to 18 hours.

2. When the first rise is complete, generously dust a work surface with bran or flour. Use a bowl scraper or rubber spatula to scrape the dough out of the bowl in one piece. Using

RECIPE CONTINUES ON NEXT PAGE

lightly floured hands or a bowl scraper or spatula, lift the edges of the dough in toward the center. Nudge and tuck in the edges of the dough to make it round.

3. Place a tea towel on your work surface, generously dust it with wheat bran or flour, and sprinkle it with ½ cup of the remaining coconut. Gently place the dough on the towel, seam side down. Lightly sprinkle the surface with the remaining ½ cup coconut. Fold the ends of the tea towel loosely over the dough to cover it and place it in a warm, draft-free spot to rise for 1 to 2 hours. The dough is ready when it is almost doubled. If you gently poke it with your finger, it should hold the impression. If it springs back, let it rise for another 15 minutes.

4. Half an hour before the end of the second rise, preheat the oven to 475 degrees F, with a rack in the lower third, and place a covered 4½- to 5½-quart heavy pot in the center of the rack.

5. Using pot holders, carefully remove the preheated pot from the oven and uncover it. Unfold the tea towel and quickly but gently invert the dough into the pot, seam side up. (Use caution—the pot will be very hot; see photos, page 55.) Cover the pot and bake for 40 minutes.

6. Remove the lid and continue baking until the bread is a deep chestnut color but not burnt, 20 to 25 minutes more.

7. Use a heatproof spatula or pot holders to carefully lift the bread out of the pot and place it on a rack to cool thoroughly.

Banana Leaf Rolls

I was in Miami Beach on vacation with my wife, Anitha, and our baby son, Declan, when the idea for this bread came to me. A few weeks earlier, I'd been disappointed by a banana bread that I was trying to concoct for this book. I often get ideas that in the end don't please me, and I discard them. In this case, the bread had turned out too cake-like, too soft. But, given my obsessiveness, I hadn't stopped thinking about it. So there I was walking around while Anitha was up in the hotel room tending to Declan, and I was staring at banana palm leaves waving in the breeze. It struck me that I could make something like a true bread, one with a sturdy crust, using not a pot but, for the sake of authenticity and a bit of flavor, a banana leaf to contain the steam. I decided not to limit myself to the flavor of bananas but to use several different palm-tree fruits. Coconuts and dates came to mind because of the complexity of flavor they would bring.

NOTE: I recommend buying frozen banana leaves, because when you thaw them, they're more pliable than fresh ones. You'll find them pretty readily in ethnic specialty stores. I can't give you a precise number of leaves to buy, because you're going to find varying sizes in each package. Just keep in mind that you'll need leaves sufficient in size to be cut into four 16-by-10-inch pieces.

YIELD: Four 6-by-4-inch rolls; ⅓ pound each
EQUIPMENT: A 4½- to 5½-quart heavy pot

INGREDIENTS	MEASURE	WEIGHT
bread flour	2 cups plus 2 tablespoons	280 grams
finely grated unsweetened coconut	½ cup	80 grams
dried dates, pitted and cut into ¼-inch pieces	10	
table salt	¼ teaspoon	3 grams
instant or other active dry yeast	¼ teaspoon	1 gram
cool (55 to 65 degrees F) water	1¼ cups	280 grams
medium banana, cut into ¼-inch cubes	1	
frozen, large banana palm leaves, thawed	up to 4	
additional flour for dusting		

RECIPE CONTINUES ON NEXT PAGE

1. In a medium bowl, stir together the flour, coconut, dates, salt, and yeast. Add the water and, using a wooden spoon or your hand, mix until you have a wet, sticky dough and no clumps of coconut, about 30 seconds. Stir in the banana. Cover the bowl and let sit at room temperature until the surface is dotted with bubbles and the dough is more than doubled in size, 12 to 18 hours.

2. When the first rise is complete, generously dust a work surface with flour. Use a bowl scraper or rubber spatula to scrape the dough out of the bowl in one piece. Fold the dough in half and cut it crosswise into 4 equal pieces.

3. With sharp scissors, cut 4 roughly 16-by-10-inch pieces from the palm leaves and carefully wipe them clean with a cloth. Place 1 leaf lengthwise on a clean work surface. Shape 1 piece of dough into a 4-inch square and place it in the center of the banana leaf. Fold the top and bottom ends of the leaf over the dough, leaving at least 2 inches of space between the edge of the dough and the fold on either side of the package, to allow room for the bread to rise. Tuck the sides of the leaf under and transfer the package to a large baking sheet. Repeat with the remaining pieces of dough. Place the rolls in a warm, draft-free spot to rise for 1 hour.

4. Preheat the oven to 500 degrees F, with a rack in the middle.

5. Place the baking sheet in the oven and bake for 25 to 35 minutes. The leaves should be very dark and just starting to char. If not, continue to bake for a few minutes longer. Remove the baking sheet from the oven and quickly but carefully unwrap each roll to prevent them from steaming. Place the rolls on a rack to cool; don't cut into them until they have cooled, about 15 minutes. If you like, return the rolls to the banana leaves to serve.

The Banana Leaf Roll Process in Pictures

1 Cutting the banana leaf. **2** Cutting the dough. **3** Wrapping the dough. **4** Presenting the finished rolls.

Jones Beach Bread

If you've read the earlier sections of this book, you know that I am fascinated by the practices of ancient and prehistoric bakers. That's why while working on this collection, one chilly, rainy day, I got in my car, drove out to Jones Beach, and strode into the freezing water with a pail. After collecting about a gallon of good old Atlantic Ocean water from the crashing waves, I got back into my car, shivering in my damp jeans, and drove to the bakery. The reason? My guess is that in the earliest days, one way of using saltwater—and not wasting the precious fresh—was to bake with it. So I tried it, and without getting too scientific, I'd say it worked great. Some people who have used my basic recipe say they like their bread a little saltier. This struck me as the slightly saltier version. In other words, the salt level in the water at Jones Beach was just fine—as it probably is at a clean beach near you, although there will always be some variation from spot to spot. I invite you to give it a shot just for the adventure of it and see how it turns out. It's all about playfulness. Your guests will get a kick out of prehistoric you; I'll bet on it.

YIELD: One 10-inch round loaf; 1¼ pounds
EQUIPMENT: A 4½- to 5½-quart heavy pot

INGREDIENTS	MEASURE	WEIGHT
bread flour	3 cups	400 grams
instant or other active dry yeast	¼ teaspoon	1 gram
seawater, passed once through a coffee filter placed in a sieve (to remove particulates like sand or algae)	1⅓ cups	300 grams
wheat bran, cornmeal, or additional flour for dusting		

1. In a medium bowl, stir together the flour and yeast. Add the seawater and, using a wooden spoon or your hand, mix until you have a wet, sticky dough, about 30 seconds. Cover the bowl and let sit at room temperature until the surface is dotted with bubbles and the dough is more than doubled in size, 12 to 18 hours.

2. When the first rise is complete, generously dust a work surface with flour. Use a bowl scraper or rubber spatula to scrape the dough out of the bowl in one piece. Using lightly floured hands or a bowl scraper, lift the edges of the dough in toward the center. Nudge and tuck in the edges of the dough to make it round.

3. Place a tea towel on your work surface and generously dust it with wheat bran, cornmeal, or flour. Gently place the dough on the towel, seam side down. If the dough is tacky, dust the top lightly with wheat bran, cornmeal, or flour. Fold the ends of the tea towel loosely over the dough to cover it and place it in a warm, draft-free spot to rise for 1 to 2 hours. The dough is ready when it is almost doubled. If you gently poke it with your finger, it should hold the impression. If it springs back, let it rise for another 15 minutes.

4. Half an hour before the end of the second rise, preheat the oven to 475 degrees F, with a rack in the lower third, and place a covered 4½- to 5½-quart heavy pot in the center of the rack.

5. Using pot holders, carefully remove the preheated pot from the oven and uncover it. Unfold the tea towel and quickly but gently invert the dough into the pot, seam side up. (Use caution—the pot will be very hot; see photos, page 55.) Cover the pot and bake for 30 minutes.

6. Remove the lid and continue baking until the bread is a deep chestnut color but not burnt, 15 to 30 minutes more. Use a heatproof spatula or pot holders to lift the bread out of the pot and place it on a rack to cool thoroughly.

VARIATION • OCEAN BREAD WITH NORI

The pieces of seaweed distributed through the bread lend it a pleasantly vegetal flavor and, since the whole point of this bread is to have some fun, give you even more to talk about with friends. You can cut the nori with a knife or scissors. In the bakery, we cut the littlest pieces with scissors.

Add 5 grams nori, finely cut or chopped (½ cup) to the mixed dough in Step 1, stirring until thoroughly incorporated.

Beyond Water
Beer, Juices, and More

For most of this book my mantra is how fundamental bread is—a dough made simply from water, salt, flour, and yeast and then baked. But I've also told you how important experimenting is to me. If you have a sense of playfulness, you can try many bread variations on your own. In this section, my intention is to offer some inspiration. My very first effort at moving away from plain old water was a dough made with beer. Other breads here incorporate fruit and vegetable juices. I introduced all of these liquids, initially, for flavor, but they also fortify the bread with nutrients. When you learn to taste flavors in your mind, the way a creative chef does, your own variations will start to come naturally. Think like a painter: the dough is your palette, with my basic method as your starting point. From there, you create the painting that appeals to you. Sometimes it will work, sometimes it won't. But you'll have fun.

Jim's Irish Brown Bread

As Italian as most of my breads are, I still find myself, an Irish boy from Long Island, drawn to traditional Irish soda bread. The usual version is a bread made with baking soda and buttermilk. I decided to intensify the Irish accent with Guinness stout. (I stayed with yeast rather than baking soda to get the dough to rise.) My bread is pungent with a hint of barley and the tartness of the buttermilk, and it's darkened to an appealing amber color by the beer and whole wheat. The Irish often add currants or raisins for a touch of sweetness, and I've included a similar variation here.

YIELD: One 10-inch round loaf; 1¼ pounds
EQUIPMENT: A 4½- to 5½-quart heavy pot

INGREDIENTS	MEASURE	WEIGHT
bread flour	2¼ cups	300 grams
whole wheat flour	¾ cup	100 grams
table salt	1 teaspoon	6 grams
wheat bran	1 tablespoon	5 grams
instant or other active dry yeast	¼ teaspoon	1 gram
Guinness stout, at room temperature (about 72 degrees F)	¾ cup	175 grams
well-shaken buttermilk, at room temperature	¾ cup	175 grams
additional wheat bran or flour for dusting		

1. In a medium bowl, stir together the flours, salt, wheat bran, and yeast. Add the beer and buttermilk and, using a wooden spoon or your hands, mix until you have a wet, sticky dough, about 30 seconds. Cover the bowl and let sit at room temperature until the surface is dotted with bubbles and the dough is more than doubled in size, 12 to 18 hours.

2. When the first rise is complete, generously dust a work surface with flour. Use a bowl scraper or rubber spatula to scrape the dough out of the bowl in one piece. Using lightly floured hands or a bowl scraper, lift the edges of the dough in toward the center. Nudge and tuck in the edges of the dough to make it round.

RECIPE CONTINUES ON NEXT PAGE

3. Place a tea towel on your work surface and generously dust it with wheat bran or flour. Gently place the dough on the towel, seam side down. If the dough is tacky, dust the top lightly with wheat bran or flour. Fold the ends of the tea towel loosely over the dough to cover it and place it in a warm, draft-free spot to rise for 1 to 2 hours. The dough is ready when it is almost doubled. If you gently poke it with your finger, it should hold the impression. If it springs back, let it rise for another 15 minutes.

4. Half an hour before the end of the second rise, preheat the oven to 475 degrees F, with a rack in the lower third, and place a covered 4½- to 5½-quart heavy pot in the center of the rack.

5. Using pot holders, carefully remove the preheated pot from the oven and uncover it. Unfold the tea towel and quickly but gently invert the dough into the pot, seam side up. (Use caution—the pot will be very hot; see photos, page 55.) Cover the pot and bake for 30 minutes.

6. Remove the lid and continue baking until the bread is a deep chestnut color but not burnt, 20 to 30 minutes more. Use a heatproof spatula or pot holders to lift the bread out of the pot and place it on a rack to cool thoroughly.

VARIATION • IRISH BROWN BREAD WITH CURRANTS

Add 150 grams (1¼ cups) currants to the flour mixture in Step 1. Increase the amounts of Guinness and buttermilk to 230 grams (1 cup) each.

Jim's Irish Brown Bread.

Carrot Bread.

Carrot Bread

One of my earliest efforts when experimenting with using juices was to enrich my basic dough with carrot juice. It seemed familiar (think of carrot cake) and exotic at the same time. It excited me to realize that a carrot bread—or, for that matter, any bread made with juice—didn't seem to exist anywhere else. The pale yellow result was beautiful, and the gentle carrot flavor was enhanced by what seemed to be a whiff of chocolate, somehow produced by the combination of carrot and currants. It was a sophisticated bread that I knew people would devour and talk about.

YIELD: One 10-inch round loaf; 1¼ pounds

EQUIPMENT: A 4½- to 5½-quart heavy pot; an extraction-type juicer is useful, but if you don't have one, you can get freshly made juice at the health food store or juice bar

INGREDIENTS	MEASURE	WEIGHT
bread flour	3 cups	400 grams
table salt	1¼ teaspoons	8 grams
instant or other active dry yeast	¼ teaspoon	1 gram
freshly squeezed carrot juice	1½ cups	350 grams
currants	¾ cup	100 grams
coarsely chopped walnuts	¾ cup	85 grams
additional flour for dusting		
cumin seeds	1 tablespoon	8 grams

1. In a medium bowl, stir together the flour, salt, and yeast. Add the carrot juice and, using a wooden spoon or your hands, mix until you have a wet, sticky dough, about 30 seconds. If it's not really sticky to the touch, add another tablespoon or two of water. Add the currants and walnuts and mix until incorporated. Cover the bowl and let sit until the surface is dotted with bubbles and the dough is more than doubled in size, 12 to 18 hours.

2. When the first rise is complete, generously dust a work surface with flour. Use a bowl scraper or rubber spatula to scrape the dough out of the bowl in one piece. Using lightly

RECIPE CONTINUES ON NEXT PAGE

floured hands or a bowl scraper, lift the edges of the dough in toward the center. Nudge and tuck in the edges of the dough to make it round.

3. Place a tea towel on your work surface. Generously dust it with flour and sprinkle on the cumin seeds. Gently place the dough on the towel, seam side down. If the dough is tacky, dust the top lightly with flour. Fold the ends of the tea towel loosely over the dough to cover it and place it in a warm, draft-free spot to rise for 1 to 2 hours. The dough is ready when it is almost doubled. If you gently poke it with your finger, it should hold the impression. If it springs back, let it rise for another 15 minutes.

4. Half an hour before the end of the second rise, preheat the oven to 450 degrees F, with a rack in the lower third, and place a covered 4½- to 5½-quart heavy pot in the center of the rack.

5. Using pot holders, carefully remove the preheated pot from the oven and uncover it. Unfold the tea towel and quickly but gently invert the dough into the pot, seam side up. (Use caution—the pot will be very hot; see photos, page 55.) Cover the pot and bake for 25 minutes.

6. Remove the lid and continue baking until the bread is a deep chestnut color but not burnt, 15 to 20 minutes more. Use a heatproof spatula or pot holders to carefully lift the bread out of the pot and place it on a rack to cool thoroughly.

Apple Bread

You can probably pretty much taste this bread in your imagination, but what I've done here is to use apples in two ways—fresh and dehydrated—to create a more unusual loaf. The dried apples become almost like an apple spread when cooked, like apple butter. The fresh chunks are more recognizable as the fruit, but less intense, like steamed apples. This bread is slightly moister than most of the other variations on the basic loaf.

YIELD: One 10-inch loaf; 1¼ pounds
EQUIPMENT: A 4½- to 5½-quart heavy pot; an extraction-type juicer is useful, but if you don't have one, you can use the unfiltered cider or apple juice available in supermarkets or buy fresh juice at a health food store or juice bar.

INGREDIENTS	MEASURE	WEIGHT
bread flour	2 cups plus 2 tablespoons	280 grams
whole wheat flour	2 tablespoons	20 grams
peeled and chopped (¼-inch cubes) Golden Delicious or Granny Smith apple	about ¾ cup	65 grams
dried apple slices, chopped into ¼-inch pieces	about 1 cup	65 grams
table salt	¾ teaspoon	4 grams
instant or other active dry yeast	¼ teaspoon	1 gram
freshly squeezed apple juice or unfiltered cider or apple juice	1 cup	250 grams
wheat bran for dusting		
thin apple slice (cut horizontally from the middle of an apple), seeds removed	1	
additional flour for dusting		

1. In a medium bowl, stir together the flours, fresh and dried apples, salt, and yeast. Add the apple juice and, using a wooden spoon or your hand, mix until you have a wet, sticky dough, about 30 seconds. Cover the bowl and let sit at room temperature until the surface is dotted with bubbles and the dough is more than doubled in size, 12 to 18 hours.

RECIPE CONTINUES ON NEXT PAGE

2. When the first rise is complete, generously dust a work surface with flour. Use a bowl scraper or rubber spatula to scrape the dough out of the bowl in one piece. Using lightly floured hands or a bowl scraper, lift the edges of the dough in toward the center. Nudge and tuck in the edges of the dough to make it round.

3. Place a tea towel on your work surface and dust it with wheat bran. Lay a piece of parchment paper slightly larger than the slice of apple in the middle of the cloth and place the apple on it (the parchment paper will prevent the wheat bran from sticking to the apple slice). Gently place the dough on the towel, seam side down, centering it on top of the apple slice. Lightly dust the top of the dough with flour. Fold the ends of the towel loosely over the dough to cover it and place it in a warm, draft-free spot to rise for 1 to 2 hours. The dough is ready when it is almost doubled. If you gently poke it with your finger, it should hold the impression. If it springs back, let it rise for another 15 minutes.

4. Half an hour before the end of the second rise, preheat the oven to 475 degrees F, with a rack in the lower third, and place a covered 4½- to 5½-quart heavy pot in the center of the rack.

5. Using pot holders, carefully remove the preheated pot from the oven and uncover it. Unfold the tea towel and quickly but gently invert the dough into the pot, so the apple slice is on the top. (Use caution—the pot will be very hot; see photos, page 55.) Remove the parchment paper. Cover the pot and bake for 45 minutes.

6. Remove the lid and continue baking until the bread is a medium chestnut color, about 10 minutes more. Use a heatproof spatula or pot holders to gently lift the bread out of the pot and place it on a rack to cool thoroughly.

Peanut Bread

First off, you've got to love peanut butter, as I always have, to appreciate this bread. It's a rich and unusual treat, the kind of thing guests won't stop talking about. If you feel the urge, go ahead and smear some jelly on it. In the recipe on page 103, I've gone all the way and incorporated the jelly directly into the bread.

YIELD: One 10-inch round loaf; 1⅓ pounds
EQUIPMENT: A 4½- to 5½-quart heavy pot

INGREDIENTS	MEASURE	WEIGHT
bread flour	2 cups plus 2 tablespoons	280 grams
whole wheat flour	2 tablespoons	20 grams
table salt	¾ teaspoon	4 grams
instant or other active dry yeast	¼ teaspoon	1 gram
cool (55 to 65 degrees F) water	1 cup plus 2 tablespoons	260 grams
unsalted smooth peanut butter	3 tablespoons	50 grams
wheat bran and additional flour for dusting		
unsalted dry-roasted peanuts, whole	¼ cup	35 grams
unsalted dry-roasted peanuts, roughly chopped	¼ cup	35 grams

1. In a medium bowl, stir together the flours, salt, and yeast. In a blender, blend the water and peanut butter (some settling will occur if this is left to stand, so blend just before using). Add to the flour mixture and, using a wooden spoon or your hand, mix until you have a wet, sticky dough without any lumps, about 30 seconds. Stir in the whole peanuts until evenly distributed. Cover the bowl and let sit at room temperature until the surface is dotted with bubbles and the dough is more than doubled in size, 12 to 18 hours.

2. When the first rise is complete, generously dust a work surface with flour. Use a bowl scraper or rubber spatula to scrape the dough out of the bowl in one piece. Using lightly floured hands or a bowl scraper, lift the edges of the dough in toward the center. Nudge and tuck in the edges of the dough to make it round.

RECIPE CONTINUES ON NEXT PAGE

3. Place a tea towel on your work surface. Generously dust it with wheat bran or flour. Gently place the dough on the towel, seam side down. Sprinkle the surface of the dough with a light dusting of flour. Fold the ends of the tea towel loosely over the dough to cover it and place it in a warm, draft-free spot to rise for 1 to 2 hours. The dough is ready when it is almost doubled. If you gently poke it with your finger, it should hold the impression. If it springs back, let it rise for another 15 minutes.

4. Half an hour before the end of the second rise, preheat the oven to 475 degrees F, with a rack in the lower third, and place a covered 4½- to 5½-quart heavy pot in the center of the rack.

5. Using pot holders, carefully remove the preheated pot from the oven and uncover it. Sprinkle half the chopped peanuts into the pot. Unfold the tea towel and quickly but gently invert the dough into the pot, seam side up. (Use caution—the pot will be very hot; see photos, page 55.) Sprinkle the remaining chopped peanuts on top of the dough. Cover the pot and bake for 45 minutes.

6. Remove the lid and continue baking until the bread is medium chestnut color, about 10 minutes. Use a heatproof spatula or pot holders to carefully lift the bread out of the pot and place it on a rack to cool thoroughly.

Peanut Butter and Jelly Bread in Pictures (recipe follows)

1 Peanuts in loaf pan. **2** The dough ready for baking.

Peanut Butter and Jelly Bread.

Peanut Butter and Jelly Bread

In this embellishment of the recipe on page 101, you get the jelly along with the peanut butter. You might think this is something just kids are going to like, but after I decided to go all the way with the combination and started offering slices to all sorts of people—adults—at the bakery, it turned out to be a huge hit with them too. It's a fascinating sweet snack. You'll notice that there is a departure here. I've forsaken my pot for an uncovered loaf pan, which results in greater softness, a desirable texture in this particular creation.

YIELD: One 8-inch loaf; 1⅓ pounds
EQUIPMENT: An 8½-by-4½-inch (6-cup) loaf pan (see Note)

INGREDIENTS	MEASURE	WEIGHT
egg, beaten	1 large	about 60 grams
bread flour	2 cups plus 2 tablespoons	280 grams
whole wheat flour	2 tablespoons	20 grams
table salt	¾ teaspoon	4 grams
instant or other active dry yeast	¼ teaspoon	1 gram
cool (55 to 65 degrees F) water	1 cup plus 2 tablespoons	260 grams
unsalted smooth peanut butter	3 tablespoons	50 grams
unsalted dry-roasted peanuts, whole	¼ cup	35 grams
unsalted dry-roasted peanuts, roughly chopped	¼ cup	35 grams
seedless fruit jam of choice	⅓ cup	100 grams
nonstick cooking spray		
additional flour for dusting		

NOTE: While many loaf pans will serve the purpose, the best by far—although it is expensive at $110—is the sturdy All-Clad. Unlike other pans, it has handles, which are a blessing when you remove it from the oven.

1. Reserve 1 tablespoon of the beaten egg for glazing the bread. In a medium bowl, stir together the flours, salt, yeast, and the remaining egg. Blend the water and peanut butter

RECIPE CONTINUES ON NEXT PAGE

in a blender until smooth (some settling will occur if this is left to stand, so blend just before using). Add mixture to the flour mixture and, using a wooden spoon or your hand, mix until you have a wet, sticky dough without any lumps, about 30 seconds. Stir in the whole peanuts until evenly distributed. Cover the bowl and let sit at room temperature until the surface is dotted with bubbles and the dough is more than doubled in size, about 12 hours.

2. When the first rise is complete, sprinkle the surface of the dough with flour. Use a bowl scraper or rubber spatula to scrape the dough out of the bowl in one piece. Lightly flour your hands and gently pat and pull the dough into a rough rectangle about 8 by 12 inches.

3. Now you're going to make a sort of jelly roll: Position the dough so a long side is in front of you. Spread the jam evenly over the surface of the dough, leaving a 1-inch border on all sides. Lift up the far side of the rectangle and fold one third of it over toward the center, then continue rolling up the remainder into a cylinder. With the seam on the bottom, tuck the ends of the roll under to seal them, so the jam doesn't ooze out during baking.

4. Lightly coat the loaf pan with cooking spray. Sprinkle half of the chopped peanuts into the bottom of the pan. Gently transfer the dough, seam side down, to the loaf pan. Sprinkle the remaining chopped peanuts onto the dough. Cover the dough with a towel and place it in a warm, draft-free spot to rise for 1 hour. The dough is ready when it has doubled. If you gently poke it with your finger, it should hold the impression. If it springs back, let it rise for another 15 minutes.

5. About 15 minutes before the end of the second rise, preheat the oven to 450 degrees F, with a rack in the center.

6. Brush the top of the dough with the reserved beaten egg. Bake until golden, about 1 hour and 15 minutes. If the peanuts start to darken, loosely cover the loaf with foil. Use pot holders to invert the pan onto a rack, remove the pan, and turn the bread right side up to cool thoroughly. (Don't dawdle—the bread will get soggy if it cools in the pan.)

The Jelly Roll Process in Pictures

1 Scraping the dough out of the bowl. **2** Spreading the dough out on the work surface. **3** The dough ready for topping.
4 Evenly spreading the jam. **5** Leaving a border on all sides. **6** Rolling the dough and jam to form a cylinder.

Almond-Apricot Bread

The almond is native to the Middle East (it's mentioned in the Bible a number of times), and it was an Israeli friend who got me thinking about it as something I might use in bread. The nut—it's actually the seed of the almond tree—is a healthful little guy, full of protein and, as you undoubtedly know already, versatile in its uses. Almonds and apricots are a natural couple, actual kin. The formal genus, *Prunus*, includes stone fruits like apricots, peaches, cherries, and plums—and almonds. It's pure harmony.

YIELD: One 8-inch round loaf; 1½ pounds
EQUIPMENT: A 4½- to 5½-quart heavy pot

INGREDIENTS	MEASURE	WEIGHT
bread flour	2 cups plus 2 tablespoons	280 grams
whole wheat flour	2 tablespoons	20 grams
quartered dried apricots	about 1⅓ cups packed	65 grams
table salt	¾ teaspoon	4 grams
instant or other active dry yeast	¼ teaspoon	1 gram
cool (55 to 65 degrees F) water	1 cup plus 2 tablespoons	260 grams
unsalted smooth almond butter	3 tablespoons	50 grams
roughly chopped almonds	3 tablespoons	35 grams
wheat bran and additional flour for dusting		

1. In a medium bowl, stir together the flours, apricots, salt, and yeast. Blend the water and almond butter in a blender (some settling will occur if this is left to stand, so blend just before using). Add to the flour mixture and, using a wooden spoon or your hand, mix until you have a wet, sticky dough without any lumps, about 30 seconds. Cover the bowl and let sit at room temperature until the surface is dotted with bubbles and the dough is more than doubled in size, 12 to 18 hours.

2. When the first rise is complete, generously dust a work surface with flour. Use a bowl scraper or rubber spatula to scrape the dough out of the bowl in one piece. Using lightly

floured hands or a bowl scraper, lift the edges of the dough in toward the center. Nudge and tuck in the edges of the dough to make it round.

3. Place a tea towel on your work surface and dust it with wheat bran and 2 tablespoons of the chopped almonds. Gently place the dough on the almonds, seam side down. Sprinkle the top of the dough with the remaining chopped almonds and a light dusting of flour. Fold the ends of the tea towel loosely over the dough to cover it and place it in a warm, draft-free spot to rise for 1 to 2 hours. The dough is ready when it is almost doubled. If you gently poke it with your finger, it should hold the impression. If it springs back, let it rise for another 15 minutes.

4. Half an hour before the end of the second rise, preheat the oven to 475 degrees F, with a rack in the lower third, and place a covered 4½- to 5½-quart heavy pot in the center of the rack.

5. Using pot holders, carefully remove the preheated pot from the oven and uncover it. Unfold the tea towel and quickly but gently invert the dough into the pot, seam side up. (Use caution—the pot will be very hot; see photos, page 55.) Cover the pot and bake for 45 minutes.

6. Remove the lid and continue baking until the bread is a deep chestnut color but not burnt, about 10 minutes more. Use a heatproof spatula or pot holders to carefully lift the bread out of the pot and place it on a rack to cool thoroughly.

Fresh Corn Bread

If you have ever ordered a typical Southern meal, like ribs or fried chicken, you've tasted the type of corn bread that comes with it, a soft, cake-like kind of thing. I have no particular beef with it, but this bread is nothing like that. The recipe is one more way to take a vegetable juice and flavor my basic bread in a fascinating, understated way.

YIELD: One 9-inch round loaf; 1 pound
EQUIPMENT: A 4½- to 5½-quart heavy pot

INGREDIENTS	MEASURE	WEIGHT
ears corn, shucked	about 4	
bread flour	2 cups plus 2 tablespoons	280 grams
fine cornmeal	2 tablespoons	20 grams
table salt	¾ teaspoon	4 grams
instant or other active dry yeast	¾ teaspoon	3 grams
additional flour and cornmeal for dusting		

1. Cut the kernels off the corncobs, and set aside 50 grams (¾ cup). Scrape the cobs over a bowl to get the remaining liquid, and transfer it to a blender. Add the remaining corn kernels, and puree until smooth. Force the puree through a fine-mesh sieve into a bowl; you should have 250 grams (1 cup) corn juice.

2. In a medium bowl, stir together the flour, cornmeal, reserved corn kernels, salt, and yeast. Add the corn juice and, using a wooden spoon or your hand, mix until you have a wet, sticky dough without any lumps, about 30 seconds. Cover the bowl and let sit at room temperature until the surface looks puffy and is more than doubled in size, 12 to 18 hours.

3. When the first rise is complete, generously dust a work surface with flour. Use a bowl scraper or rubber spatula to scrape the dough out of the bowl in one piece. Using lightly

floured hands or a bowl scraper, lift the edges of the dough in toward the center. Nudge and tuck in the edges of the dough to make it round. Allow the dough to settle for 5 minutes.

4. Place a tea towel on your work surface and generously dust it with cornmeal. Gently place the dough on the towel, seam side down. If the dough is tacky, dust the top lightly with cornmeal. Fold the ends of the tea towel loosely over the dough to cover it and place it in a warm, draft-free spot to rise for 1 to 2 hours. The dough is ready when it is almost doubled. If you gently poke it with your finger, it should hold the impression. If it springs back, let it rise for another 15 minutes.

5. Half an hour before the end of the second rise, preheat the oven to 450 degrees F, with a rack in the lower third, and place a covered 4½- to 5½-quart heavy pot in the center of the rack.

6. Using pot holders, carefully remove the preheated pot from the oven and uncover it. Unfold the tea towel and quickly but gently invert the dough into the pot, seam side up. (Use caution—the pot will be very hot; see photos, page 55.) Cover the pot and bake for 45 minutes.

7. Remove the lid and continue baking until the bread is a medium chestnut color, about 10 minutes. Use a heatproof spatula or pot holders to gently lift the bread out of the pot and place it on a rack to cool thoroughly.

Fennel-Raisin Bread

This may be the most unusual of my breads. It was inspired by a fennel-and-raisin loaf at Amy's Bread in Manhattan, but I thought, why stop there? I decided to add fennel juice too, to replace the water and intensify the flavor. The result is the essence of fennel—not overpowering, but distinct. This recipe requires more planning than most of the others, since the fennel has to be candied and then requires 12 hours to dry before being mixed into the dough. Yet even though there's more work involved, I'm sure you'll find it's worth it. (You'll want to eat it soon, as the bread won't keep for more than a day.)

YIELD: One 10-inch round loaf; 1½ pounds
EQUIPMENT: A 4½- to 5½ quart heavy pot and an extraction-type juicer

INGREDIENTS	MEASURE	WEIGHT
fennel bulbs with stalks and fronds	2 medium	1 kilogram
cool (55 to 65 degrees F) water	1 cup	225 grams
sugar	1 cup	190 grams
bread flour	2 cups plus 2 tablespoons	280 grams
whole wheat flour	2 tablespoons	20 grams
table salt	¾ teaspoon	4 grams
instant or other active dry yeast	¼ teaspoon	1 gram
Sambuca, Pernod, or other anise-flavored liqueur	1 teaspoon	5 grams
golden raisins	¾ cup	125 grams
roughly chopped almonds	⅓ cup	40 grams
wheat bran and additional flour for dusting		
fennel seeds	2 tablespoons	16 grams

1. Trim the stalks from 1 fennel bulb (reserve the remaining fennel bulb and stalk) and cut twenty ¼-inch cubes from the stalks; set aside.

2. Combine the water and sugar in a small pot and bring to a simmer, stirring until the sugar is dissolved. Add the fennel stalk pieces and simmer for 3 to 5 minutes, until soft. Drain the candied fennel and spread on a parchment- or wax-paper-lined baking sheet. Let dry in a cool, dry place for at least 12 hours.

3. When the candied fennel is dry and you're ready to mix the dough, cut the reserved fennel bulb and stalk into pieces that will fit into the juicer feed tube. Juice enough fennel to yield 1 cup plus 2 tablespoons.

4. In a medium bowl, stir together the flours, salt, and yeast. Add the fennel juice and Sambuca and, using a wooden spoon or your hand, mix until you have a wet, sticky dough without any lumps, about 30 seconds. Stir in the raisins, almonds, and candied fennel until evenly distributed. Cover the bowl and let sit at room temperature until the surface is dotted with bubbles and the dough is more than doubled in size, about 12 hours.

5. When the first rise is complete, generously dust a work surface with flour. Use a bowl scraper or rubber spatula to scrape the dough of the bowl in one piece. Using lightly floured hands or a bowl scraper, lift the edges of the dough in toward the center. Nudge and tuck in the edges of the dough to make it round.

6. Place a tea towel on your work surface. Generously dust it with wheat bran and half the fennel seeds. Gently place the dough on the towel, seam side down. Sprinkle the surface of the dough with the remaining fennel seeds and a light dusting of flour. Fold the ends of the towel loosely over the dough to cover it and place it in a warm, draft-free spot to rise for 1 to 2 hours. The dough is ready when it is almost doubled. If you gently poke it with your finger, it should hold the impression. If it springs back, let it rise for another 15 minutes.

7. Half an hour before the end of the second rise, preheat the oven to 450 degrees F, with a rack in the lower third, and place a covered 4½- to 5½-quart heavy pot in the center of the rack.

8. Using pot holders, carefully remove the preheated pot from the oven and uncover it. Unfold the tea towel and quickly but gently invert the dough into the pot, seam side up. (Use caution—the pot will be very hot; see photos, page 55.) Cover the pot and bake for 45 minutes.

9. Remove the lid and continue baking until the bread is a medium chestnut color, about 10 minutes. Use a heatproof spatula or pot holders to gently lift the bread out of the pot and place it on a rack to cool thoroughly.

Pizza Bianca (page 137).

CHAPTER 4

Pizzas and Focaccias

In the United States, pizzas often seem like some species of their own, a completely different breed of thing from bread. In Italy, pizza and bread are more sensibly recognized as cousins. It's the most natural thing in the world for a bread maker to bake and sell pizza as well, just as that same baker may offer sandwiches. In both cases, it is, in a way, a matter of dressing the bread. And, unlike the versions you see in America, in Italy, pizza toppings are often stunningly simple and light.

Basic Pizza Dough

Many of my pizzas are created with this dough as the foundation. Although it's similar in some ways to my basic bread recipe, this dense, brittle, thin pizza base (it's slightly sweet once it's baked and browned) is more about the toppings than achieving a rich bread flavor. So this versatile dough uses more yeast than my basic bread does, because I'm not interested in a particularly long period of fermentation here. I'm not looking for the expansion or the light texture and rich flavor of a good loaf of bread (rather, it should be thin and crisp), and I want to hurry it up—the first rise takes just 2 (rather than 12 to 18) hours. The sugar in the recipe is to feed the yeast. It helps jump-start it. One variation you may notice as you move from recipe to recipe is in the time each pizza takes to bake—because the toppings vary quite a bit, some cook faster than others.

This recipe makes enough dough for two 13-by-18-inch pies (each can be cut into 8 rectangular slices), but the recipes specifying various toppings yield only one pizza each. I've done it this way because most people seem to want variety when they're serving pizza, you can bake one of this and one of that. If you're only going to bake one pizza, it's a simple matter to halve the dough recipe (using a scale, that is; by volume, you'll have to approximate somewhat). You could also make the full recipe and refrigerate half the dough in a lightly oiled freezer bag for up to 1 day, or freeze it for up to 1 month, well wrapped. Thaw the still-wrapped frozen dough overnight in the refrigerator and bring it to room temperature before shaping the pie.

YIELD: Enough dough for two 13-by-18-inch pies
EQUIPMENT: Two 13-by-18-inch rimmed baking sheets

INGREDIENTS	MEASURE	WEIGHT
bread flour	3¾ cups	500 grams
instant or other active dry yeast	2½ teaspoons	10 grams
table salt	¾ teaspoon	5 grams
sugar	¾ teaspoon plus a pinch	about 3 grams
room-temperature (about 72 degrees F) water	1⅓ cups	300 grams
extra virgin olive oil for the pans		

RECIPE CONTINUES ON NEXT PAGE

1. In a medium bowl, stir together the flour, yeast, salt, and sugar. Add the water and, using a wooden spoon or your hand, mix until blended, at least 30 seconds. The dough is a bit stiffer than most of the others in this book, not as wet and sticky. Cover the bowl and let sit at room temperature until the dough has more than doubled in volume, about 2 hours.

2. Using a bowl scraper or rubber spatula, remove the dough from the bowl onto a floured work surface. Gently form into a rough ball. Then divide the dough into two halves, spacing them 4 inches apart, and cover both with a moistened kitchen towel for 30 minutes.

3. When you are ready to make your pie, oil two 13-by-18-inch rimmed baking sheets. Pick up the dough and invert and stretch the dough the length of the baking sheet. The floured side should now be facing up and the moist side should now be on the pan. Using your palms, gently pull, press, and stretch the dough to fill the entire bottom of the pan. There is no need to make a crust or a lip around the edge of the pan. Your objective should be to make an even layer of dough across the entire bottom of the pan. If the dough sticks to your fingers, lightly dust it with flour or coat your hands with oil. Pinch any holes together. Repeat with the second piece. The dough is ready to top as you like (see the following recipes).

Basic Pizza Dough in Pictures

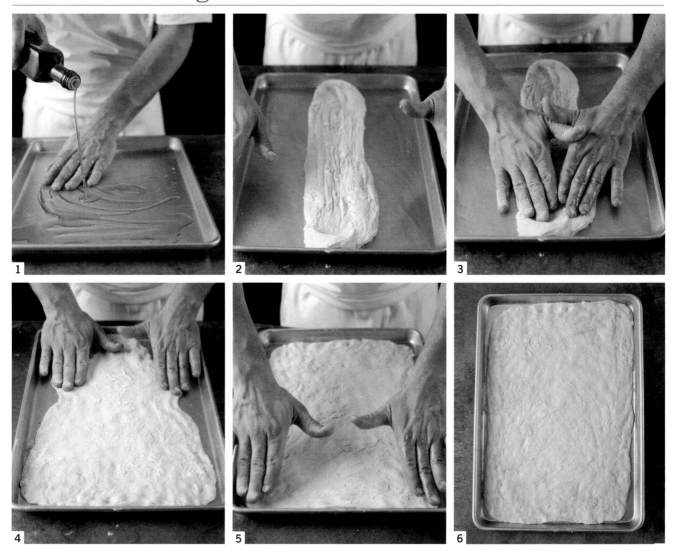

1 Oiling a baking sheet. **2** The dough pulled to fill the baking sheet. **3** Pressing the dough evenly. **4** Stretching the dough out to fill the sheet. **5** Pressing the dough to the edges. **6** The dough ready for topping.

Pizza Pomodoro • TOMATO PIZZA

I make my tomato sauce especially moist so that it will not reduce and become too concentrated and sweet tasting as the pizza bakes. As simple as this pizza is, it has an intense, pure taste, with the tomato alone as the star. If you want to spice it up a bit turn to the variation that follows, Pizza Amatriciana, which is named after the town of Amatrice north of Rome, known for its tomato sauce with pancetta.

YIELD: One 13-by-18-inch pie; 8 slices

INGREDIENTS	MEASURE	WEIGHT
can of your favorite diced tomatoes in juice, drained	one 14½-ounce can	411 grams
juice of the canned tomatoes reserved	¾ cup	175 grams
extra virgin olive oil	1½ teaspoons	8 grams
table salt	¼ teaspoons	3 grams
Basic Pizza Dough (page 117)	½ recipe	400 grams

1. Preheat the oven to 500 degrees F, with a rack in the center.

2. Use a blender, food processor, or immersion blender to pulse together the tomatoes with the reserved juice, the olive oil, and salt until they are chunky. The mixture will be very liquid.

3. With a ladle or large spoon, spread the tomato sauce evenly over the dough, going all the way to the edges. Don't let the sauce pool in the middle or in any other spot; actually, you want the sauce to be a bit thicker everywhere but the middle because the edges tend to cook and brown more quickly.

4. Bake for 25 to 30 minutes, until the edges are slightly charred and the crust is pulling away from the sides of the pan. Serve the pizza hot or at room temperature.

Scatter 8 very thin slices of pancetta, 55 grams (about ¼ cup) thinly sliced onion, and 1 gram (½ teaspoon) crushed red pepper flakes over the pizza before baking.

Preparing to Bake the Pizza Pomodoro

1 Oiling a baking sheet. **2** The dough ready for topping.

SLICING PIZZA

All of my pizzas (except Pizza Bianca) are prepared in 13-by-18-inch pans. While you can serve them in slices of any size you like, at the bakery we find that rectangles of about 3 by 4 inches are ideal. They make for a satisfying portion and are easy to handle. You start by cutting the pizza in half, then quartering it, and finally cutting each quarter in half.

A chef's knife will do this job well, but if you fail to control the knife with a steady hand, the result may be just a little uneven. There are two other options. One is the pizza wheel you see in every pizza restaurant. A wheel with a standard 4-inch blade should cost about $15. It allows you to roll through the pizza straight and fast. At the bakery, though, we use a tool called a mezzaluna. The name refers to the shape of the blade, which resembles a half-moon (*mezza* is Italian for "half," *luna* means "moon"). The classic ones come with a handle mounted on either side of the blade, and you use a rocking motion (think of a rocking chair) to do the cutting. Mostly these blades are used to chop herbs, but a mezzaluna makes the job of slicing a pizza extremely easy. Rock it just once or twice, and you've made a smooth long cut. In the bakery we use a big one, with a 20-inch blade, but that's probably too cumbersome to store in your kitchen. A perfectly serviceable 11-inch mezzaluna will cost just $20 or so and doesn't pose the storage problem. Just be sure to get the single-blade style, not one with two parallel blades, which, of course, would make a mess of the job.

THE THIN SLICE

In many of my recipes, I tell you to slice the ingredients very thin. One reason that's so for pizzas is that the toppings need to cook quickly. Thin slices are also delicate and fresh tasting, the way thick slices can never be. And thin slices—whether on a pizza or in a sandwich—won't produce what I call overload. In other words, they won't overwhelm the creation but rather blend in, while still adding their own distinct flavors.

When I specify a certain thickness in a recipe, I know you may not achieve it exactly. For the most part, the measurements I provide are

Pizza equipment: **1** mezzaluna; **2** bread knife; **3** plastic spatula; **4** salt; **5** box grater; **6** pie plate; **7** peel; **8** pizza stone.

Pizza equipment: 1 small chef's knife; 2 wooden spoons; 3 mandoline; 4 round pizza cutter; 5 brushes; 6 Foley food mill; 7 cooling rack.

meant as guidelines. You'll need to use a sharp chef's knife for meats (or, as in the case of paper-thin prosciutto, have the professional at the store do it). But for vegetables, a knife won't produce the uniformity required for even cooking and good looks, and you'll have a hard time getting the really thin slices ($\frac{1}{16}$ inch) that you can produce so easily with a device known as a mandoline, my vegetable slicer of choice. A mandoline, if you're unfamiliar with it, looks a bit like a washboard. You slide the vegetable along its surface until it strikes the (very sharp) blade, and each slice falls out below. It got its name, or so the story goes, when a chef described his rapid slicing motion as strumming. But I don't want you thinking so casually. You're going to need a finger guard—often sold along with the tool—or a protective blade-resistant glove. If you slice bare-handed and too fast, I guarantee you will cut yourself.

There are countless mandolines on the market, some with steel bodies, some with plastic bodies—most have stainless steel blades—and most will do an acceptable job. The more expensive ones usually have stable folding legs. You need to support most other versions in one hand while slicing with the other, or rest them on a bowl. Just make sure whatever you buy is easily adjustable for thickness. They range in price from the big, sturdy, sharp Japanese Shun mandoline, which costs an astronomical $400, to the smaller Kyocera, with an unusual ceramic blade, that goes for about $25. For the vegetable slicing in these recipes, the size of the slicer won't make any difference. The Kyocera draws raves from home cooks and some chefs (it's simple to adjust, wash, and store), though chefs sometimes feel they have to hide it in the kitchen because it is little and colorful and looks like a toy compared to, for instance, the all-time classic, the French Bron mandoline (about $200, but often on sale for less), in glistening stainless steel. At the bakery, I use one of the popular Japanese mandolines made by Benriner, and I've always found it was up to the task at hand. These cost from $30 to $50, depending on size. I'm fond of mine, but I see by a few reviews on the web that some people find the finger guard flimsy—so it seems that, for the nonprofessional, blade-resistant protective gloves would be useful.

Pizza Funghi • MUSHROOM PIZZA

This pizza was inspired by a visit to the restaurant Pó in New York City, when Mario Batali was still the chef in the kitchen. The moment I tried his terrific risotto with mushrooms, onions, and thyme, it struck me that the combination would make a superb pizza topping. You'll notice the slices of mushroom are very thin: thicker slices would release too much liquid on the surface of the pizza. Also, because the thin slices dry out quickly, they become pleasantly crispy.

YIELD: One 13-by-18-inch pie; 8 slices
EQUIPMENT: A mandoline

INGREDIENTS	MEASURE	WEIGHT
cremini mushrooms, trimmed	1¼ pounds	550 grams
diced yellow onion	1⅓ cups	133 grams
fresh thyme leaves	2 teaspoons	1 gram
Basic Pizza Dough (page 117)	½ recipe	400 grams
table salt	1 teaspoon	6 grams
extra virgin olive oil	2½ tablespoons	40 grams

1. Preheat the oven to 500 degrees F, with a rack in the center.

2. Use a mandoline to cut the mushrooms into thin slices (⅛ inch thick). In a medium bowl or on the pan, toss together the mushrooms, onion, and thyme.

3. Scatter or spread the mushroom mixture fairly evenly over the dough, going all the way to the edges; put a bit more of the topping around the edges of the pie, as the outside tends to cook and brown more quickly. Sprinkle with the salt and drizzle with the olive oil.

4. Bake for 25 to 30 minutes, until the mushrooms are starting to turn golden brown and the crust is pulling away from the sides of the pan. Serve the pizza hot or at room temperature.

Pizza Funghi in Pictures

1 The dough ready for topping. **2** Tossing together the mushrooms, onion, and thyme. **3** Spreading the mixture over the dough.
4 Sprinkling salt over the pizza. **5** Drizzling oil over the pizza. **6** The finished pizza.

Pizza Cavolfiore • CAULIFLOWER PIZZA

This pizza, like the Pizza Funghi (page 126), was inspired by an incredible dish—this time it was a pasta with roasted cauliflower, bread crumbs, and olives (cooked by the chef Sarah Jenkins). It's another classic Italian combo, but not one typically found on a pizza. The cheese you use here should be of the highest quality—it makes a difference.

YIELD: One 13-by-18-inch pie; 8 slices
EQUIPMENT: A mandoline

INGREDIENTS	MEASURE	WEIGHT
cauliflower, outermost green leaves removed	1 medium	700 grams
finely chopped pitted Sicilian colossal or other large green olives	just under ½ cup	60 grams
freshly grated Parmigiano-Reggiano or Grana Padano	about ½ cup	60 grams
garlic, finely grated or very finely minced	2 large cloves	15 grams
table salt	¾ teaspoon	4 grams
crushed red pepper flakes	½ teaspoon or to taste	1 gram
extra virgin olive oil	¼ cup	60 grams
Basic Pizza Dough (page 117)	½ recipe	400 grams
Homemade Bread Crumbs (page 211)	1 to 2 tablespoons	10 to 15 grams

1. Preheat the oven to 500 degrees F, with a rack in the center.

2. Cut the cauliflower into quarters. Using a mandoline, shave it into very thin slices (about ¹⁄₁₆ inch thick). In a medium bowl, toss together the cauliflower, olives, Parmesan, garlic, salt, red pepper flakes, and olive oil.

3. Spread the cauliflower mixture over the dough, going all the way to the edges; put a bit more of the topping around the edges of the pie, as the outside tends to cook and brown more quickly. Sprinkle evenly with the bread crumbs.

4. Bake for 25 to 30 minutes, until the topping is starting to turn golden brown and the crust is pulling away from the sides of the pan. Serve the pizza hot or at room temperature.

Pizza Patate • POTATO PIZZA

Potato pizza is another Italian classic you don't see very often in the United States. While my rendition is pretty traditional, I soak the potatoes in salted water first, which actually extracts about 20 percent of their moisture. That causes them to cook more quickly and makes them firmer. It's a little trick I learned from cooking potato pancakes.

YIELD: One 13-by-18-inch pie; 8 slices
EQUIPMENT: A mandoline

INGREDIENTS	MEASURE	WEIGHT
lukewarm water	1 quart	800 grams
table salt	4 teaspoons	24 grams
Yukon Gold potatoes, peeled	6 to 8	1 kilo
diced yellow onion	1 cup	100 grams
freshly ground black pepper	½ teaspoon	2 grams
extra virgin olive oil	about ⅓ cup	80 grams
Basic Pizza Dough (page 117)	½ recipe	400 grams
fresh rosemary leaves	about 1 tablespoon	2 grams

1. Preheat the oven to 500 degrees F, with a rack in the center.

2. In a medium bowl, combine the water and salt, stirring until the salt is dissolved. Use a mandoline to slice the potatoes very thin (¹⁄₁₆ inch thick), and put the slices directly into the salted water so they don't oxidize and turn brown. Let soak in the brine for

RECIPE CONTINUES ON NEXT PAGE

1½ hours (or refrigerate and soak for up to 12 hours), until the slices are wilted and no longer crisp.

3. Drain the potatoes in a colander and use your hands to press out as much water as possible, then pat dry. In a medium bowl, toss together the potato slices, onion, pepper, and olive oil.

4. Spread the potato mixture evenly over the dough, going all the way to the edges of the pan; put a bit more of the topping around the edges of the pie, as the outside tends to cook more quickly. Sprinkle evenly with the rosemary.

5. Bake for 30 to 35 minutes, until the topping is starting to turn golden brown and the crust is pulling away from the sides of the pan. Serve the pizza hot or at room temperature.

VARIATION • PIZZA BATATA (SWEET POTATO PIZZA)

Substitute 2 sweet potatoes (800 grams), peeled, for the Yukon Gold potatoes, and use about 4½ cups (about 900 grams) water and 24 grams (4 teaspoons) salt for the soaking liquid. Omit the rosemary in the topping.

Pizza Patate.

Pizza Zucchine • ZUCCHINI PIZZA

This is very close to a traditional pizza you'll find in many towns and cities in Italy, but I substitute Gruyère for the Fontina used in Italy. I love the sweet, nutty tang it adds. I also like to add bread crumbs, preferably homemade, which bring a wonderful crunch to what is otherwise a fairly soft topping.

YIELD: One 13-by-18-inch pie; 8 slices

INGREDIENTS	MEASURE	WEIGHT
trimmed zucchini	2½ pounds; about 3 large	1.2 kilos
table salt	1½ teaspoons	10 grams
grated Gruyère or high-quality Swiss cheese	2 cups	150 grams
Basic Pizza Dough (page 117)	½ recipe	400 grams
Homemade Bread Crumbs (page 211)	2 to 2½ tablespoons	20 to 25 grams

1. Preheat the oven to 500 degrees F, with a rack in the center.

2. Use a food processor with a grater attachment or a box grater to grate the zucchini. In a medium bowl, toss together the zucchini and salt. Let stand for 15 to 20 minutes, until the zucchini has wilted and released its water.

3. Drain the zucchini in a colander, then use your hands to squeeze out as much water as possible, then pat dry. In a medium bowl, toss together the zucchini and cheese, breaking up any clumps of zucchini, until well mixed.

4. Spread the zucchini mixture over the dough, going all the way to the edges of the pan; put a bit more of the topping around the edges of the pie, as the outside tends to cook and brown more quickly. Sprinkle evenly with the bread crumbs.

5. Bake for 25 to 30 minutes, until the topping is starting to turn golden brown and the crust is pulling away from the sides of the pan. Serve the pizza hot or at room temperature.

Pizza Radici di Sedano • CELERY ROOT PIZZA

After I perfected my potato pizza, I found myself wondering what other root vegetables might work in the same way. I had just eaten a celery root puree at a restaurant and realized that its sweet flavor, which I find has a hint of anise, would be wonderful as a topping. As the pizza bakes, the slices of celery root soften almost to the point of creaminess.

YIELD: One 13-by-18-inch pie; 8 slices
EQUIPMENT: A mandoline

INGREDIENTS	MEASURE	WEIGHT
celery root	4 to 6 bulbs	800 grams
diced yellow onion	⅓ cup	33 grams
table salt	¾ teaspoon	4 grams
extra virgin olive oil	about ⅓ cup	80 grams
Basic Pizza Dough (page 117)	½ recipe	400 grams
freshly grated nutmeg	1 teaspoon	6 grams
or		
ground nutmeg	¼ teaspoon	2 grams

1. Preheat the oven to 500 degrees F, with a rack in the center.

2. Peel the celery root and use a mandoline to slice it very thin (¹⁄₁₆ inch thick). In a medium bowl, toss together the celery root, onion, salt, and olive oil.

3. Spread the celery root mixture over the dough, going all the way to the edges; put a bit more of the topping around the edges of the pie, as the outside tends to cook and brown more quickly. Sprinkle with the nutmeg.

4. Bake for 25 to 30 minutes, until the topping is starting to turn golden brown and the crust is pulling away from the sides of the pan. Serve the pizza hot or at room temperature.

Pizza Cipolla • ONION PIZZA

On its face, this may seem to be the most ordinary of the pizzas present here. But if you've seen all my passing references to the ancients in this book, you'll get one reason for it being included. The onion is in fact a prehistoric food, just like bread, and it was common, even glorified, in ancient Egypt. The name itself comes from the Latin word, *unio*, "unity." These days, the onion is taken for granted. But embraced in a cream base as it is in this recipe, it's far from ordinary.

YIELD: One 13-by-18-inch pie; 8 slices
EQUIPMENT: A mandoline

INGREDIENTS	MEASURE	WEIGHT
yellow onions	2 medium	650 grams
heavy cream	⅓ cup	80 grams
table salt	1 teaspoon	6 grams
fresh thyme leaves, coarsely chopped	2 teaspoons	1 gram
Basic Pizza Dough (page 117)	½ recipe	400 grams

1. Preheat the oven to 500 degrees F, with a rack in the center.

2. Use a mandoline to cut the onions into thin slices (⅛ inch thick); you want about 6 cups sliced onion. In a medium bowl, toss together the onion slices, heavy cream, salt, and thyme.

3. Spread the onion mixture evenly over the dough going all the way to the edges; put a bit more topping around the edge of the pie, as the outside tends to cook more quickly.

4. Bake for 30 to 35 minutes, until the topping is starting to turn golden brown and the crust is pulling away from the sides of the pan. Serve the pizza hot or at room temperature.

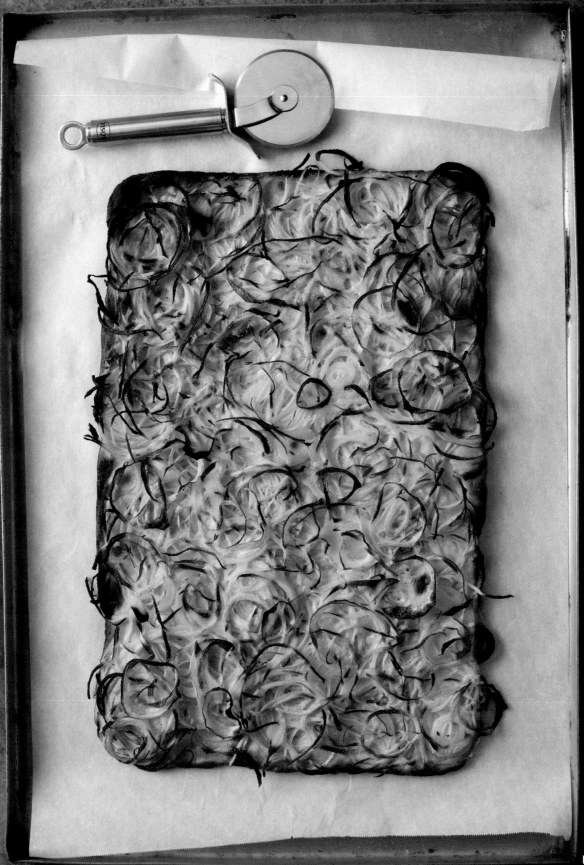

Pizza Cipolla.

Pizza Bianca in Pictures

1 Dusting a peel with flour. 2 Placing the dough on the peel. 3 Dimpling the dough and pouring in oil. 4 Dimpling the remaining dough. 5 Loosening the dough. 6 Putting on the rosemary. 7 The finished Pizza Bianca.

Pizza Bianca

Bianca in Italian means "white," which is not exactly what a pizza bianca is. "Almost naked" might be a better description, as it is one of the least adorned pizzas. It's pretty much a flatbread that you flavor with good olive oil (unlike my basic pizza dough) and often some herbs. I use rosemary leaves here, but any fresh herb or combination that appeals to you will work. And that's it. In Rome, pizza bianca is eaten in the morning, the way Americans eat buttered toast—and then throughout the day, too, because Romans never seem to be able to get enough of a really wonderful, simple thing. Notice that this pizza is not made on a baking sheet, as the others are, but is baked on a stone and requires a peel to get it in and out of the oven. Both the peel ($20 or so) and stone (usually around $25) are quite inexpensive; they are available in kitchen stores and on the Internet (through Amazon, among other sources).

YIELD: One 14-inch pie; 6 to 8 slices
EQUIPMENT: A large (at least 14 inches in diameter) pizza stone and a pizza peel

INGREDIENTS	MEASURE	WEIGHT
bread flour, plus additional for dusting	3 cups	400 grams
instant or other active dry yeast	¼ teaspoon	1 gram
table salt	½ teaspoon	4 grams
sugar	¾ teaspoon	4 grams
cool (55 to 65 degrees F) water	1½ cups	350 grams
extra virgin olive oil, plus additional for coating the bowl and brushing	¼ cup	60 grams
coarse sea salt	½ teaspoon	4 grams
fresh rosemary, leaves removed	3 sprigs	

1. In a medium bowl, stir together the flour, yeast, table salt, and sugar. Add the water and, using a wooden spoon or your hand, mix until you have a wet, sticky dough, about 30 seconds. Lightly coat a second medium bowl with olive oil and place the dough in it. Cover the bowl and let sit at room temperature, until the surface is dotted with bubbles and the

RECIPE CONTINUES ON NEXT PAGE

dough is more than doubled in size, 9 to 12 hours. (While most of the breads in this book can rise for as long as 18 hours, this one is at the short end of the range because a longer rise would cause the dough to be less elastic, more firm, and it needs to be stretched out.)

2. When the first rise is complete, generously dust a work surface (a cutting board is useful here) with flour. Use a bowl scraper or rubber spatula to scrape the dough out of the bowl in one piece; as you begin to pull it away from the bowl, it will cling in long, thin strands and will be quite loose and sticky. Using lightly floured hands, fold the dough over itself two or three times and nudge it into a loose, rather flat ball. Brush the surface of the dough with olive oil and sprinkle with the coarse salt (which will gradually dissolve on the surface). Put the dough in a warm, draft-free spot and let rise until doubled, 1 to 2 hours.

3. Half an hour before the end of the second rise, preheat the oven to 500 degrees F, with a rack in the center, and place a pizza stone, at least 14 inches in diameter, in the center of the rack.

4. Generously dust a pizza peel with flour and place the ball of dough in the middle. Spread out the fingers of one hand, like a claw, and drive your fingers into the dough, but do not puncture it (short nails are essential; see photos, page 136): you want to simultaneously create dimples in the dough and spread it out across the peel. Continue working your hand across the dough and dimpling it until you have a bumpy disk about 12 inches in diameter. Drizzle the remaining olive oil over the top and sprinkle with the rosemary leaves.

5. With the peel resting on the counter (this part gets easier with practice), grasp the handle and give it a quick little tug: you want the pizza to just barely move but stay on the peel. (Loosening it makes it easier to slide it onto the baking stone.) If the dough sticks to the peel, gently lift it around the edges and add flour to the peel. Shake the pizza onto the baking stone. Bake for 12 to 15 minutes, until the crust is golden brown on the mounds but still pale in the dimples.

6. Slide the peel under the pizza and transfer it to a rack to cool for at least a few minutes before slicing and serving.

VARIATION • SCHICCIATA D'UVA (SWEET RAISIN AND GRAPE PIZZA)

After scraping the dough out onto the work surface in Step 2, scatter about 10 grams (1 heaping tablespoon) raisins over the surface of the dough. Then proceed by folding the dough and brushing it with olive oil, but sprinkle it with 2 tablespoons (25 grams) sugar instead of the coarse salt. In Step 4, begin to dimple and stretch out the dough. Halfway through the dimpling process, spread 300 grams (about 3 cups) small stemmed champagne grapes (or if you do not mind grape seeds, you can use Concord or wine grapes) over the dough, drizzle the remaining olive oil over the top, and continue dimpling, smashing some of the grapes into the dough as you do so. Sprinkle with 6 grams (about 2 teaspoons) anise seeds and 1 tablespoon sugar. Bake as directed.

Pizza Finocchio • FENNEL PIZZA

If you tried my fennel bread (page 112), you have an idea about how much I love the plant. I don't think this is a topping you'll find at your local pizzeria, no matter how "famous" or "original" the name says it is (as they so often proclaim in New York City).

YIELD: One 13-by-18-inch pie; 8 slices
EQUIPMENT: A mandoline

INGREDIENTS	MEASURE	WEIGHT
trimmed fennel bulbs	2 medium	650 grams
freshly grated Parmigiano-Reggiano or Grana Padano	⅓ cup loosely packed	about 40 grams
table salt	¾ teaspoon	4 grams
freshly ground black pepper	¼ teaspoon	1 gram
extra virgin olive oil	about ¼ cup	60 grams
Basic Pizza Dough (page 117)	½ recipe	400 grams

1. Preheat the oven to 500 degrees F, with a rack in the center.

2. Use a mandoline to cut the fennel into very thin slices (about ¹⁄₁₆ inch thick); you want about 7 cups sliced fennel. In a medium bowl, toss together the fennel, cheese, salt, pepper, and olive oil.

3. Spread the fennel mixture over the dough going all the way to the edges; put a bit more of the topping around the edge of the pie, as the outside tends to cook and brown more quickly.

4. Bake for 30 to 35 minutes, until the topping is starting to turn golden brown and the crust is pulling away from the sides of the pan. Serve the pizza hot or at room temperature.

Focaccia

Focaccia and pizza are close cousins, but focaccia is lighter and thicker, about 1½ inches, rather than dense and thin. In this recipe, I replace some of the flour and water in my basic pizza dough with a boiled potato (as soft as you can get it, without having it fall apart). This helps lighten the dough. Focaccia can be served plain, but it allows for quite a bit of creativity in how it's flavored with various toppings (particularly, just about any fresh herb), so I encourage you to use this and the recipe that follows as a formula for your own whims.

YIELD: One 13-by-18-inch focaccia
EQUIPMENT: A 13-by-18-inch rimmed baking sheet

INGREDIENTS	MEASURE	WEIGHT
peeled Yukon Gold potato, cut into 1-inch chunks	about 1 cup	200 grams
cool (55 to 65 degrees F) water	2½ cups	600 grams
bread flour	4½ cups	600 grams
instant or other active dry yeast	2½ teaspoons	10 grams
sugar	1 teaspoon	4 grams
table salt	1½ teaspoons	10 grams
extra virgin olive oil or grapeseed oil	¼ cup	60 grams

1. Put the potatoes and water in a small saucepan, cover, and bring to a boil over high heat. Cook until the potato chunks fall apart when pierced with a fork or knife tip.

2. Use a blender, an immersion blender, or a food mill to puree the potatoes with the cooking water until smooth. Let the mixture cool to 120 degrees F; it will feel very warm to the touch but not scalding.

3. In a large bowl, stir together the flour, yeast, sugar, and half the salt. Add the potato puree and, using a wooden spoon or your hands, mix until you have a wet, sticky dough, about

RECIPE CONTINUES ON NEXT PAGE

30 seconds. Cover the bowl and let sit at room temperature until the dough is tripled in size, 2 to 3 hours.

4. Lightly oil a 13-by-18-inch rimmed baking sheet. Use a bowl scraper or rubber spatula to scrape the dough onto the baking pan; it will still be quite loose and sticky. Gently pull the dough and stretch it across the surface of the pan, then oil your hands and press the dough evenly out to the edges. Drizzle with 3 tablespoons of the oil and sprinkle with the remaining salt. Use your fingertips to create dimples all over the surface of the dough. Let the dough rise in a warm, draft-free spot until it has risen just over the edges of the pan, 45 minutes to 1 hour.

5. Half an hour before the end of the second rise, preheat the oven to 400 degrees F, with a rack in the center.

6. Gently place the focaccia in the oven on the center rack (the risen dough is delicate; a bump going into the oven could collapse it) and bake for 30 to 45 minutes, until the top is evenly golden brown. Transfer the pan to a rack to cool, and give it at least a few minutes before slicing and serving warm or at room temperature.

Focaccia.

Focaccia Dolce • SWEET FOCACCIA

The sweetness here comes from a great combination of dried fruits, sugar, and honey. Sweet focaccia is one of the traditional snack foods of Italy; it's not a bad breakfast, either. The ingredients can vary, of course: this particular version was inspired by Paula Oland, the baker at Balthazar in New York City.

YIELD: One 13-by-18-inch focaccia
EQUIPMENT: A 13-by-18-inch rimmed baking sheet

INGREDIENTS	MEASURE	WEIGHT
chopped dried apricots	⅓ cup	40 grams
raisins	⅓ cup	40 grams
dried cherries	⅓ cup	40 grams
roughly chopped dried figs	⅓ cup	40 grams
roughly chopped pitted dates	⅓ cup	40 grams
dry white wine or water	½ cup	100 grams
bread flour	3 cups	400 grams
sugar	½ cup	95 grams
table salt	¾ teaspoon	4 grams
instant or other active dry yeast	2 teaspoons	8 grams
room-temperature (72 degrees F) water	⅔ cup	150 grams
eggs, at room temperature, beaten	2 large	about 100 grams
honey	1 tablespoon	25 grams
unsalted butter, softened, plus more for coating the bowl	4 tablespoons (½ stick)	57 grams
apricot jam	½ cup	150 grams
sliced almonds (use untoasted almonds; they'll toast during baking)	about 1¾ cups	150 grams
powdered sugar	⅓ cup	45 grams

1. Put all the fruit in a bowl and pour in the white wine or water. Let soak overnight, or until most of the liquid is absorbed, stirring occasionally; you want the fruit to plump up a bit. Drain off any excess liquid.

2. In a medium bowl, stir together the flour, sugar, salt, and yeast. Add the water, eggs, and honey and, using a wooden spoon, mix until a soft dough forms, about 30 seconds. Stir in the butter and soaked dried fruit and continue mixing until incorporated. Lightly coat a second bowl with butter and place the dough in it. Cover and let rise at room temperature until more than doubled in size, about 8 hours.

3. Lightly butter a 13-by-18-inch rimmed baking sheet. Use a bowl scraper or rubber spatula to scrape the dough onto the pan in one piece; it will still be quite loose and sticky. Gently pull the dough across the surface of the pan, then flour your hands and press the dough evenly out to the edges. Use a spatula to spread the apricot jam evenly over the dough. (At this point, you can wrap it in plastic wrap and refrigerate for up to 12 hours.)

4. In a small bowl, toss together the almonds, powdered sugar, and 1 tablespoon water until the almonds are coated with sugar (add another tablespoon of water if necessary to coat them). Scatter the almonds evenly over the top of the focaccia. Let the dough rise in a warm, draft-free spot until it has risen just to the edges of the pan, about 3 hours.

5. Half an hour before the end of the second rise, preheat the oven to 400 degrees F, with a rack in the center.

6. Bake the focaccia on the center rack for 25 to 30 minutes, until the top is golden brown. Transfer the pan to a rack to cool, and give it at least 10 minutes before slicing and serving warm or at room temperature.

The "Speckeroni" (page 185).

CHAPTER 5

The Art of the Sandwich

In the early days, when my bakery was still on Sullivan Street, I learned about a guy they called the Sandwich Nazi (named after the *Seinfeld* Soup Nazi character, of course). He was a moody, irritable, intolerant perfectionist, a genuine artist named Alessandro Gualandro, and his shop was called Melampo (under new ownership, it is now called Alidoro). Gualandro would not be rushed as he layered—ever so lightly—each simple ingredient onto his beautifully baked and sliced bread. The meats and cheeses were always cut by hand. A little mozzarella, some prosciutto di Parma, a bit of arugula. Not fancy, but perfect.

Great bread by itself is something like a grand piano alone on the stage. The sandwich is the piano joined by an orchestra. I try to hold on to that Italian sandwich tradition, the artistry of it, as best I can. Sometimes, I feel more like a sushi chef than anything else. What I'm striving for, just like Alessandro Gualandro before me, is lightness, balance, and a burst of flavor. The sandwiches in this chapter are nothing like the pound of sliced turkey and coleslaw on rye that comes to mind when one thinks of American sandwiches. For me, a sandwich is all about flavors complementing each other—and about the bread itself. Thin layers of ingredients working together in harmony. I'm aiming for sandwiches that will sing in your mouth, not fill you up. The sandwiches of the Sullivan Street Bakery are almost as much a part of the place as the loaves of bread on the shelves behind them.

To create a terrific sandwich, first taste the ingredients in your mind, then go for it, one thin layer at a time. The foundation, often the meat or cheese, is the platform to hold the rest. As you layer, contemplate how each ingredient will feel and taste against the others. Take a familiar example, a ham sandwich with lettuce: you wouldn't put the mustard on the lettuce side, because it would affect the crunchy texture and do nothing good for the overall taste; instead you want the tartness of the mustard to meld with the richness of the ham. Of course, once you start chomping on a well-made sandwich, much of the artistry may not matter, but you want the first bites, like the first sip of wine, to set the tone, to be perfect.

Sometimes one of my sandwiches will have a star—the tomato, for instance—and everything about it will be there to intensify that ingredient: the herbs, the cheese, the dressing. In the sandwich I call the "PMB" (pancetta, mango, and basil, page 182), the mango, with its unexpectedly sweet juiciness, is the star. Other times I want you to taste all the ingredients as one—my Panino di Melanzane (eggplant and red peppers, page 178) is an example of this. A good principle to keep in mind, along with the need to strive for lightness and beauty, is that just about any time you think of a well-composed salad, you have the ingredients for a sandwich, with the brilliant, brittle addition of really good crackling bread.

Whenever feasible, I prepare the ingredients myself. Most store-bought food, even some of the best, is compromised by processing and by the fact that it's been sitting around. In the first section of this chapter, you'll find recipes for making many of the components of my favorite sandwiches at home. Since you're starting with the incredible bread you've made yourself, it's worth extending your efforts to the filling as well. True, there's nothing especially terrible about roast beef from a deli, but just try my Rosemary Roast Beef (page 150), and you'll see how incredibly different two roast beef sandwiches can be. And since so many condiments are easy to make yourself, it just seems like a shame to go to the local supermarket for a jar.

Homemade Sandwich Ingredients

Rosemary Roast Beef

This is the perfect roast beef for building a perfect sandwich. I start with an eye-round roast, which is a compact cut but I like to tie it anyway to make it neater and tighter. I'm looking for a certain density for slicing. I also find the act of tying a roast in a meticulous way to be sort of therapeutic, like meditation, and maybe you will too; you'll find illustrated instructions on page 154. Another touch is that I roast it in a skillet, not a roasting pan. This allows me to sear it on the stovetop and then roast it in the same pan.

YIELD: One 4-pound roast

EQUIPMENT: A heavy ovenproof skillet large enough to hold the roast, an instant-read thermometer, and kitchen twine

INGREDIENTS	MEASURE	WEIGHT
finely chopped fresh rosemary	2 tablespoons	8 grams
table salt	1 tablespoon	18 grams
coarsely ground black pepper	1 tablespoon	14 grams
sugar	¼ teaspoon	1 gram
eye-round beef roast	one 4-pound	1.8 kilos
grapeseed oil or canola oil	about ¼ cup or as needed	45 grams or as needed

1. Preheat the oven to 300 degrees F.

2. In a small bowl, mix together the rosemary, salt, pepper, and sugar. Sprinkle the mixture all over the beef, rubbing it into the meat. Use kitchen twine to tie the beef so it maintains a round shape (see "How to Tie a Roast," page 154).

3. Heat an ovenproof skillet large enough to hold the beef easily over medium-high heat for a minute or two. Add 2 tablespoons of the oil, then add the beef and sear on all sides until well browned, about 3 minutes per side; add more oil by the tablespoon as you turn the beef if the pan seems dry.

4. Transfer the pan to the oven. For rare, as I prefer it, roast until the internal temperature reads 110 to 120 degrees F, about 1¼ hours.

5. Transfer the beef to a cutting board or platter, cover with foil lightly, and let rest for at least 25 minutes. Or cool to room temperature, then wrap in plastic, and refrigerate for up to 3 days. Thinly slice just before serving.

For the Panino di Manzo (Roast Beef Sandwich with Aioli), page 173.

Citrus Roast Pork

The outdated notion that pork must be cooked to well-done before it is safe still causes many people to feel uncomfortable with pork that is actually perfectly cooked—that is, moist, tender, and delicious. Relax and be assured that a little rosiness in the center is fine (and desirable) so long as the roast reaches the internal temperature specified. I call for removing the roast from the oven at 130 degrees F and letting it rest for 25 minutes; it will rise to about 145 degrees F while resting (leave the thermometer in place to be sure it's reached the correct temperature).

I make a deep slit in the roast and insert lemon zest and garlic, a bright combination that will permeate the meat. (See illustrations on page 155.)

YIELD: One 4-pound pork roast
EQUIPMENT: An instant-read thermometer and kitchen twine

INGREDIENTS	MEASURE	WEIGHT
boneless pork, top loin roast	one 4-pound	1.8 kilos
finely grated lemon zest	1 teaspoon	2 grams
finely chopped garlic	1 teaspoon	2 grams
table salt	1 tablespoon	24 grams
freshly ground black pepper	1 teaspoon	4 grams
grapeseed oil or canola oil	about 1 tablespoon or as needed	10 grams or as needed

1. Preheat the oven to 350 degrees F.

2. In a small bowl, mix together the lemon zest, garlic, 1 teaspoon of the salt, and the pepper. Lay the pork on a cutting board fat side down. Starting from a long side, slice halfway through the roast, without cutting all the way through. Sprinkle the lemon zest mixture over the top of the pork and into the center, rubbing it into the meat. Use kitchen twine to tie the pork so it maintains its shape (see "How to Tie a Roast," page 154).

3. Rub the pork with just enough oil to coat it and sprinkle it with the remaining 2 teaspoons salt. Put it fat side up in a roasting pan large enough to hold it comfortably. Roast until the internal temperature is 130 to 140 degrees F, 1 to 1¼ hours.

4. Transfer the pork to a cutting board or platter and let rest for 25 minutes. Or cool to room temperature, then wrap in plastic and refrigerate for up to 3 days. Thinly slice just before serving.

For the Panino Cubano (Cuban Sandwich), page 174.

Ingredients for Citrus Roast Pork.

HOW TO TIE A ROAST

The meat is easier to handle if you pat it dry with paper towels. For the best shape, make sure your knots are evenly spaced and in a straight line down the roast.

1. Cut a generous length of kitchen twine, about nine times the length of the roast.

2. Roll the meat into as even a log shape as possible.

3. Tie a slipknot at one end of the twine and loop the other end through it; put this loop over one end of the meat, about 1½ inches from the end.

4. Pull the twine taut so it fits snugly on the roast. It shouldn't cut into the meat, but it should be snug enough that it won't slide around.

5. Pull the end of the twine straight down an inch from the first knot and hold it in place with your index finger, then loop the end of the twine under the roast and up around the other side, keeping the loop perfectly parallel to the previous loop.

6. Pull the end under the L of the twine where your index finger is, and pull the twine taut. Repeat the process, making perfectly even, straight, tight ties around the roast, until you come to within an inch of the other end.

7. Tie the last loop with an additional knot to secure it, and trim off the excess twine.

Citrus Roast Pork in Pictures

1 A 4-pound pork roast. **2** Cutting halfway through. **3** Sprinkling the roast with pepper. **4** The seasoned roast. **5** Rolling the roast into a log shape. **6** Pulling twine tight over the roast. **7** Tying a knot in the twine. **8** The tied roast.

Jim's Aioli

One way to make aioli, a garlic mayo, is with oil, garlic, lemon juice, and egg yolk. The yolk creates an emulsion, stabilizing the tiny droplets of the oil that are suspended in the liquid to yield a thick, creamy texture that won't quickly separate (as oil and vinegar, for example, tend to do). But an equally valid approach relies on the emulsifying powers of pureed garlic, without the egg yolk. I prefer this more basic aioli—it has a purer flavor. It is as much Italian as Spanish, and the inspiration came from some time I spent on Ibiza in the Balearic Islands. The coarse salt helps break down the garlic; table salt, which dissolves more quickly, is used for the final seasoning.

YIELD: About 1 cup

INGREDIENTS	MEASURE	WEIGHT
garlic, coarsely chopped	6 medium cloves	about 30 grams
coarse sea salt	½ teaspoon	2 grams
grapeseed oil or canola oil (see Note)	¾ cup	150 grams
freshly squeezed lemon juice	2 tablespoons	40 grams
table salt	¼ teaspoon, or to taste	2 grams, or to taste

1. Puree the garlic and coarse salt in a food processor. With the machine running, slowly drizzle in the oil, processing until the mixture is thick and pale. Add the lemon juice and pulse until combined, then pulse in the table salt. The consistency should resemble mayonnaise.

2. Store in a jar or other airtight container in the refrigerator. The aioli will keep for about 4 days.

NOTE: For this recipe, I like to use a neutral-tasting oil like grapeseed or canola. But this is going on your sandwich, and if you'd like a touch of olive fruitiness, go ahead and use up to 1 tablespoon olive oil in place of some of the grapeseed.

For the Panino di Manzo (Roast Beef Sandwich with Aioli), page 173, the Panino Cubano (Cuban Sandwich), page 174, and the Panino Frittata (Omelette Sandwich), page 186.

Homemade Pickles

I find most jarred pickles too mushy and sweet for sandwiches. True, you can find very good, freshly made pickles at some delicatessens, but preparing them yourself is simple and fun. Much of what we eat is a vestige of the days before refrigeration, and pickling, of course, is an ancient form of preservation. Try it—you might get hooked.

YIELD: About 4 pounds
EQUIPMENT: Four 1-quart wide-mouth Ball jars, sterilized in boiling water for 30 seconds

INGREDIENTS	MEASURE	WEIGHT
water	2 quarts	1.6 kilos
red wine vinegar	1 cup plus 2 tablespoons	220 grams
coriander seeds	¼ cup	20 grams
garlic, peeled	6 medium cloves	about 30 grams
table salt	⅓ cup	85 grams
Kirby cucumbers	8 medium	2 kilos

1. Combine the water, vinegar, coriander, garlic, and salt in a large bowl, stirring until the salt is dissolved.

2. Wash the cucumbers well and remove any blemishes with a paring knife. Pack the cucumbers into four sterilized Ball jars. Cover the cucumbers with brine and seal tightly. Refrigerate and let cure for 2 weeks, turning the jars over occasionally.

3. Always use clean tongs to retrieve the pickles (not your hands, which would contaminate the liquid). To test if they are ready, cut one open; it should have a translucency all the way through and that typical pickle crispness and flavor. The pickles will keep in the refrigerator for a month—make sure they are submerged in the brine.

For the Panino Cubano (Cuban Sandwich), page 174.

Homemade Spicy Mustard

It's amazing how easy it is to make your own mustard, and how good it is. Since it isn't heat-pasteurized in the jar as commercial mustard is, it has a purer flavor. But unlike store-bought mustard, this stuff won't last forever. It does keep for about a month, though, and you may well find yourself ready to make another batch before then. Note that you first have to soak the seeds overnight.

YIELD: About ¾ cup

INGREDIENTS	MEASURE	WEIGHT
mustard seeds	¼ cup	45 grams
spring water	½ cup or additional to taste	100 grams or additional to taste
red wine vinegar	1 tablespoon or to taste	15 grams or to taste
table salt	¾ teaspoon or to taste	5 grams or to taste

1. Put the mustard seeds in a small bowl and cover with ¼ cup of the spring water. Let soak overnight in the refrigerator.

2. Drain any liquid from the mustard seeds and place them in a blender. Add the vinegar, salt, and the remaining ¼ cup water and puree until a paste forms; the mustard will be grainy. Add more water by the tablespoon if the mustard is too thick. Use immediately, or cover and store in the refrigerator.

For the Panino Cubano (Cuban Sandwich), page 174.

Artichoke Confit

The confit method of preserving food, slow-cooking it in oil, is perfect for baby artichokes. The oil mellows their bitterness, leaving them tender and gentle on the palate. Using baby artichokes is convenient since they have no chokes for you to worry about.

YIELD: About 3 cups

INGREDIENTS	MEASURE	WEIGHT
water	about 2 quarts	1.6 kilos
lemons, halved	2	
baby artichokes	about 10	about 550 grams
extra virgin olive oil	about 3 cups or as needed	750 grams or as needed
red wine vinegar	⅓ cup plus 1 tablespoon or to taste	75 grams or to taste
table salt	1 teaspoon or to taste	6 grams or to taste

1. Put the water in a large bowl. Squeeze the lemon juice into it and add the lemon halves. Add the artichokes; keep them in this acidulated water whenever you are not working with them—it will prevent them from browning. Remove 1 artichoke and pull off the tough outer green leaves until you reach the tender yellow ones; leave the stem intact. Use a vegetable peeler or paring knife to remove any dark (green or black) spots from the yellow inner leaves. Cut off the prickly tops, and peel off the thick outer layer from the stem. Occasionally dip the artichoke in the lemon water as you cut it to prevent discoloration. Immediately return it to the lemon water when you are finished, and repeat with the remaining artichokes.

2. Drain the artichokes well, put them in a medium heavy saucepan, and add the olive oil; use enough oil to cover the artichokes completely. Turn the heat to medium and bring the oil to a very gentle simmer. Cook for 5 minutes, then turn off the heat and let cool to

RECIPE CONTINUES ON NEXT PAGE

room temperature. The artichokes can be used immediately or refrigerated in a covered container, submerged in their oil, for up to a month.

3. About 20 minutes before serving, drain the artichokes in a colander (reserve the oil for another use, such as salad dressing, if desired). Transfer the artichokes to a medium bowl and mash them with a fork (or transfer to a board and finely chop them). Sprinkle with the vinegar and salt and mix well. Taste and adjust the seasoning with more vinegar or salt if necessary. Use immediately, or store in a covered container in the refrigerator for up to a day.

For the Panino di Carciofi e Prosciutto Cotto (Artichoke and Ham Sandwich), page 176.

Marinated Eggplant

Serve this dressed eggplant on a little plate with some cheese and roasted red pepper (page 165), and you have an appetizer. Place the same things on bread and you have a sandwich for lunch. I've got a nice bit of cilantro in this recipe, which you might be surprised to learn is a typically Roman addition.

YIELD: About 16 pieces

INGREDIENTS	MEASURE	WEIGHT
Japanese eggplant, trimmed and halved lengthwise	about 2	1 kilo
coarse sea salt	1½ teaspoons	5 grams
finely grated or chopped garlic	3 medium cloves	10 grams
chopped fresh cilantro	about 1 tablespoon	2 grams
crushed red pepper flakes	about 2 teaspoons or to taste	about 2 grams or to taste
red wine vinegar	¼ cup	60 grams
extra virgin olive oil	about 2 cups or as needed	400 grams or as needed

1. Preheat the oven to 500 degrees F.

2. Lay the eggplant halves cut side up on a large baking sheet—it's okay if the pieces are touching, but don't overlap them. Sprinkle with the coarse salt. Roast until the eggplant is soft and the skin is brown and wrinkled—somewhere between chewy and somewhat dry—about 45 minutes. Let cool to room temperature.

3. Layer half of the eggplant in an 8-inch round glass or ceramic dish, without overlapping, and sprinkle with half of the garlic, cilantro, red pepper flakes, and vinegar. Repeat layering and seasoning the remaining eggplant. Cover the eggplant with the olive oil. Cover the dish and marinate the eggplant in the refrigerator for at least 12 hours (the eggplant can marinate for up to 5 days). This dish may sound very oily, but it turns out to be only slightly so and I like what oil does remain so I don't even drain it before serving.

For the Panino di Melanzane (Eggplant Sandwich with Roasted Red Pepper), page 178; also used in Spicy Eggplant Spread, page 166.

Marinated Beets

Marinated beets are a sour-sweet ingredient you could fall in love with even on their own, but when they're combined with other ingredients in a sandwich, they really sing. The most important thing about this recipe is getting the texture right—the beets should not be so soft they're mushy, but you want to be able to pierce them easily with a knife, without meeting much resistance.

YIELD: About 3 cups
EQUIPMENT: An 8-inch round cake pan

INGREDIENTS	MEASURE	WEIGHT
scrubbed and trimmed medium beets	about 2 bunches	800 grams
red wine vinegar	6 tablespoons	85 grams
table salt	1½ teaspoons or to taste	12 grams or to taste
thinly sliced red onion	about 1 cup	about 100 grams

1. Preheat the oven to 500 degrees F.

2. Cut the tops off the beets, making a flat surface. Stand the beets in an 8-inch round cake pan with the root ends sticking up. Fill the pan with enough water to cover the beets halfway. Roast until a knife easily pierces the beets through the middle, 1 to 1¼ hours. Let cool to room temperature.

3. In a medium bowl, combine the vinegar and salt. Submerge the onion slices in the vinegar mixture. Set aside.

4. When the beets are cool, rub off the skins. Slice the beets ¼ inch thick, add to the marinade, and toss well. Cover and marinate at room temperature for at least 4 hours, or in the refrigerator for at least 12 hours.

5. Taste the beets and add salt and/or vinegar if necessary. They'll keep in the refrigerator for up to 5 days.

For the Panino de Barbietola (Beet Sandwich with Goat Cheese), page 181.

Panino di Manzo (page 173).

Marinated Sun-Dried Tomatoes

One reason to prepare your own marinated sun-dried tomatoes is that you get a chance to control the texture. If sun-dried tomatoes soak up too much water, they can become too soggy for a sandwich, but if you make them at home, you can drain the blanched tomatoes as soon as they plump.

YIELD: About 60 pieces

INGREDIENTS	MEASURE	WEIGHT
sun-dried tomatoes (not packed in oil)	about 20	100 grams
fresh rosemary needles (optional)	about 2 teaspoons	1 gram
extra virgin olive oil	1½ cups or as needed	360 grams or as needed

1. Fill a 2-quart saucepan with water and bring it to a boil. Add the tomatoes and blanch for just 30 seconds, or until plump; drain immediately. Lay the tomatoes out on paper towels or a clean kitchen towel to drain, and cool to room temperature, then pat dry.

2. Transfer the tomatoes to an airtight container or glass jar. Add the rosemary, if using, and olive oil to cover. Cover and marinate at room temperature for 12 hours.

3. The tomatoes can be used immediately or stored in the refrigerator for up to a month. Ten minutes or so before you're ready to use them, put them in a colander to drain off the oil. (The oil may bead up in the refrigerator, but that's no cause for concern.)

For the Panino di Manzo (Roast Beef Sandwich with Aioli), page 173; also used in Spicy Eggplant Spread, page 166.

Roasted Red Peppers

Most home cooks have roasted a red pepper at one time or another. My reason for always roasting and skinning them is that they become tender and marry well with other ingredients. Homemade, they are fresher, more flavorful, and more vibrant than the ones you buy in the store.

YIELD: 3 peppers

INGREDIENTS	MEASURE	WEIGHT
red bell peppers	3	

1. Preheat the oven to 500 degrees F.

2. Put the peppers on a baking sheet and roast, turning once or twice, until the skins are blistered and charred and the peppers are starting to collapse, about 30 minutes. Transfer to a bowl and let stand until cool enough to handle.

3. Peel the skins off the peppers with your fingers, or use a paper towel. Do not rinse them. Cut or tear the peppers in half and remove the stems and seeds. Use immediately, or refrigerate in a covered container for up to 5 days.

For the Panino di Melanzane (Eggplant Sandwich with Roasted Red Pepper), page 178, the "Speckeroni" (Speck with Pecorino Sandwich), page 185, and the Panino Frittata (Omelette Sandwich), page 186; also used in Spicy Eggplant Spread, page 166.

Spicy Eggplant Spread

This spread begins with a few slices each of my Marinated Eggplant (page 160), Marinated Sun-Dried Tomatoes (page 164), and Roasted Red Peppers (page 165). I particularly love a little of it on a mozzarella and ham sandwich. Because it really packs a punch, it is best used as an accent, a spicy highlight, just as you would mustard.

YIELD: About 1 cup

INGREDIENTS	MEASURE	WEIGHT
Marinated Eggplant (page 160), drained and finely chopped	4 pieces	115 grams
Marinated Sun-Dried Tomatoes (page 164), drained and finely chopped	4 pieces	20 grams
Roasted Red Pepper (page 165), finely chopped	1	20 grams
chopped fresh cilantro	just under ½ teaspoon or to taste	3 grams or to taste
crushed red pepper flakes	½ teaspoon or to taste	1 gram or to taste
red wine vinegar	about 1½ tablespoons or to taste	20 grams or to taste
crumbled dried thyme	½ teaspoon	3 grams
crumbled dried Italian oregano	½ teaspoon	3 grams

1. In a medium bowl, mix all the ingredients together. Taste and adjust the seasoning with more salt, red pepper, and or vinegar if necessary. Use immediately, or cover and store in the refrigerator for up to 5 days.

For the Panino di Mozzarella (Mozzarella Sandwich with Eggplant Spread), page 179, and the "Speckeroni" (Speck with Pecorino Sandwich), page 185.

Lemon Dressing

This bright-tasting dressing, made rich with the savory addition of anchovies, is another illustration of how nicely what could have been part of a salad, when piled between slices of good bread, morphs into a great sandwich. The recipe makes more than you'll probably need for sandwiches alone, so you could skip the bread and use this wherever a dressing is called for.

YIELD: About 1¾ cups

INGREDIENTS	MEASURE	WEIGHT
freshly squeezed lemon juice	⅓ cup, from about 2 large lemons	80 grams
chopped shallots	about ¼ cup	30 grams
oil-packed anchovies, drained and patted dry	about 3 fillets	12 grams
table salt	¾ teaspoon	4 grams
freshly ground black pepper	¼ teaspoon	1 gram
extra virgin olive oil	1⅓ cups	280 grams

1. In a food processor, combine the lemon juice, shallots, anchovies, salt, and pepper and puree until smooth. With the motor running, gradually drizzle in the olive oil so that it combines smoothly (emulsifies) with the other ingredients. Use immediately, or store in a tightly sealed jar in the refrigerator for up to 5 days. Shake the jar well before using if the dressing has separated.

For the Panino di Bresaola (Dried Beef Sandwich with Arugula), page 180.

Green Onion Bagna Cauda • GREEN ONION, ANCHOVY, AND GARLIC SAUCE

Bagna cauda (its name means "hot bath" in Italian), most strongly associated with the Piedmont region, is a warm dip, full of anchovies and garlic, that is served sort of like fondue. I use it as a sandwich ingredient, of course. When I was developing this recipe, it was the springtime, and I couldn't resist using ramps, wild green-topped onions that have a savory, garlicky punch and proliferate in the farmers' market at that time of year. I called the sandwich a "Rampwich," using the bagna cauda to dress a sliced duck egg and cheese. But since ramps are not always available, and I want you to be able to make this sauce all year round, I created a basic recipe with green onions (aka scallions), which are terrific here too, and offer the ramp version as a variation you can try when you're lucky enough to get them.

YIELD: About ¾ cup

INGREDIENTS	MEASURE	WEIGHT
unsalted butter	4 tablespoons	55 grams
extra virgin olive oil	¼ cup	60 grams
oil-packed anchovies, drained and patted dry	about 3 fillets	12 grams
green onions, trimmed, leaving most of the green part, and cut on the bias into ¼-inch pieces	1 bunch (about 1½ cups)	100 grams
table salt	⅛ teaspoon or to taste	1 gram or to taste

1. Combine the butter and olive oil in a small saucepan and turn the heat to medium. When the butter has melted, add the anchovies, green onions, and salt and cook, stirring occasionally, until the anchovies disintegrate, 15 to 20 minutes. Set aside to cool.

2. Taste the sauce and adjust the seasoning with more salt if necessary. Use immediately, or store in the refrigerator for up to 3 days.

Substitute ramps for the green onions.

For the "Rampwich" (Green Onion Bagna Cauda, Mozzarella, and Duck Egg Sandwich), page 184.

Frittata Patate • POTATO OMELETTE

The French omelette, when done according to long-established culinary rules, is a delicate, moist creation. Its cousin in Italy is a much more rustic dish, a flat, usually well-done version that can contain almost anything, from vegetables to meats. The one I've come up with was designed for a sandwich (although there's nothing to stop you from eating it without the bread) that will be topped with peppers and arugula. So I wanted to keep the eggs uncomplicated and light—incorporating only thinly sliced seasoned potatoes. The most common approach is to start a frittata on the rangetop and then finish it in the oven. But since I cook and sell it in my bakery, it turned out to be simpler to bake it entirely in the oven. It's a successful approach, as you'll see.

YIELD: One 10-inch-round, about ½-inch-thick frittata

EQUIPMENT: Mandoline and a 10-inch cast-iron or other ovenproof skillet

INGREDIENTS	MEASURE	WEIGHT
grapeseed or canola oil	2 teaspoons	6 grams
Yukon Gold potato, cut into ¹⁄₁₆-inch-thick slices	about 2 cups	250 grams
chopped Spanish onion	½ cup	50 grams
extra virgin olive oil	1 tablespoon plus 2 teaspoons	20 grams
table salt	2 teaspoons	12 grams
freshly ground black pepper	2 teaspoons	8 grams
fresh rosemary leaves	about 1 tablespoon	2 grams
eggs	4 large	about 240 grams

1. Preheat the oven to 500 degrees F. Drizzle 1 teaspoon of the grapeseed or canola oil in a well-seasoned 10-inch cast-iron or other ovenproof skillet.

2. In a medium bowl, combine the potato slices, onion, olive oil, salt, pepper, and rosemary until the potato slices are completely coated with oil and no longer stick together.

3. Arrange the potato mixture in the prepared skillet in an even layer (a few slices may overlap). Bake for 20 to 22 minutes, until the edges of the potato slices turn golden brown.

4. Transfer the potato mixture to a small bowl. Reduce the oven temperature to 400 degrees F. Add the remaining teaspoon of grapeseed or canola oil to the skillet and return to the oven for about 2 minutes to heat the oil.

5. In a medium bowl, whisk the eggs until they begin to foam, about 30 seconds. Stir in the potato mixture. Pour the egg-potato mixture into the skillet, using a wooden spoon to smooth out the top and distribute the potato slices evenly.

6. Bake for 6 to 8 minutes, until the middle is just set. Using a wooden spoon or offset spatula, loosen the edges and flip the frittata onto a paper towel–lined plate. Allow the frittata to rest for 2 to 3 minutes to drain any excess oil.

For the Panino Fritatta (Omelette Sandwich), page 186.

Panini • The Sandwiches

Now for the sandwiches. Stecca (page 75) or Stirato (page 78) are the bread choices for all these sandwiches. In the bakery, I generally go with the stecca because I prefer the somewhat less assertive crust. The glaze of oil and salt on the surface adds a bit of character. But you may prefer the stirato. If you do use a stirato, keep in mind that it has more crumb than the stecca. After you slice it, scrape out some of the interior with your fingers to allow the filling to sit there comfortably. The stecca, cut in half, will yield sandwiches about 6 inches long. The stirato, halved, will also give you two 6-inch sandwiches.

Panino di Manzo • ROAST BEEF SANDWICH WITH AIOLI

This recipe is a fine example of how fresh, well-balanced ingredients combine to create a perfect sandwich: a few slices of meat, layered on a crusty loaf and accented with fresh arugula and homemade condiments, completely recast—even revolutionize—the traditional roast beef sandwich.

YIELD: 2 sandwiches

INGREDIENTS	MEASURE	WEIGHT
Stecca (page 77) or Stirato (page 79), cut in two and split		
Jim's Aioli (page 156)	2 tablespoons	28 grams
Marinated Sun-Dried Tomatoes (page 164), drained	8 pieces	25 grams
Rosemary Roast Beef (page 150)	5 to 6 very thin slices	70 grams
arugula leaves	about ¼ cup	20 grams

1. Spread half the aioli on the bottom of each sandwich, then layer with the sun-dried tomatoes, followed by the roast beef, and finally the arugula. Serve immediately.

Panino Cubano • CUBAN SANDWICH

This is my homage to the beloved Cuban sandwich, a ham, roast pork, and cheese melt with pickles. I don't heat my version in a sandwich press (or overstuff it), so it's delicate and bright. Any sandwich of meat and cheese needs crunch, and the pickles here deliver that big-time. My aioli is not egg-based the way mayonnaise is, so when I wanted some creaminess in this sandwich, I added a bit of ordinary mayo along with the aioli.

YIELD: 2 sandwiches

INGREDIENTS	MEASURE	WEIGHT
Stecca (page 77) or Stirato (page 79), cut in two and split		
Homemade Spicy Mustard (page 158)	2 tablespoons	30 grams
Jim's Aioli (page 156)	1 tablespoon	14 grams
mayonnaise, commercial or homemade	2 teaspoons	6 grams
Gruyère, thinly sliced	about 4 slices	40 grams
prosciutto di Parma	2 paper-thin slices	
Citrus Roast Pork (page 152), sliced as thin as possible	10 slices	60 grams
Homemade Pickles (page 157), sliced lengthwise as thin as possible	4 slices	25 grams

1. Spread the mustard on the bottom halves of the sandwiches, and spread the aioli and mayonnaise on the top halves. Layer each sandwich with half of the cheese, prosciutto, roast pork, and pickles. Serve immediately.

Panino Cubano.

Panino di Carciofi e Prosciutto Cotto •
ARTICHOKE AND HAM SANDWICH

With its distinctive flavors, this sandwich has the pleasing contrasts of a simple antipasto plate. I use Crucolo, a buttery Italian cow's-milk cheese. You're looking for a flavorful soft cheese to add creaminess to the sandwich. Prosciutto cotto, Italian boiled ham, is mild and moist. Combined with the artichoke confit, the ham and cheese form an intriguing amalgam with a sour-sweet taste and a bit of muskiness.

YIELD: 2 sandwiches

INGREDIENTS	MEASURE	WEIGHT
Stecca (page 77) or Stirato (page 79), cut in two and split		
Crucolo cheese	2 tablespoons	30 grams
drained and mashed Artichoke Confit (page 159)	about ¼ cup	40 grams
prosciutto cotto, sliced as thin as possible		50 grams

1. Spread (or layer) half the cheese on the bottom half of each sandwich, and spread the artichoke confit on the top halves. Layer with the prosciutto cotto, and serve immediately.

Panino di Caprese • MOZZARELLA AND TOMATO SANDWICH

Ask me to name a single favorite sandwich, and I'm in trouble, but press on and I'll tell you this familiar combo of mozzarella, tomato, and fresh basil is probably it. When the components are all top-notch, there's nothing better, which is why this arrangement shows up as an appetizer everywhere. Adding a great bread to make it a sandwich just highlights the other ingredients. The tomato plays the central role here, with everything else supporting it, so this is definitely a seasonal sandwich.

YIELD: 2 sandwiches

INGREDIENTS	MEASURE	WEIGHT
buffalo mozzarella	about six ¼-inch slices	140 grams
perfectly ripe heirloom or other tomato, cored	1 medium	140 grams
Stecca (page 77) or Stirato (page 79), cut in two and split		
fresh basil leaves	6 medium	about 3 grams
table salt	pinch	about 1 gram
extra virgin olive oil	2 teaspoons	10 grams

1. Drain the mozzarella in a colander for 1 hour at room temperature.

2. Slice the cheese and tomato about ¼ inch thick. You'll need to cut them to fit the sandwiches neatly in one layer.

3. Layer each sandwich with half the mozzarella, tomato, and basil leaves. Sprinkle with the salt and drizzle with the olive oil. Serve immediately.

Panino di Melanzane • EGGPLANT SANDWICH
WITH ROASTED RED PEPPER

I will never forget a day during my first trip to Tuscany when I found myself wandering around a small town, feeling hungry and poor, until I stumbled upon the one shop that stayed open in the middle of the day (most close for a couple of hours right at lunchtime so everyone can go home, leaving tourists in a bind). This was the sandwich I had there: cheese, eggplant, and pepper. It was cheap, and damned good.

YIELD: 2 sandwiches

INGREDIENTS	MEASURE	WEIGHT
Stecca (page 77) or Stirato (page 79), cut in two and split		
aged pecorino Toscano or other pecorino	2 thin slices	about 20 grams
Marinated Eggplant (page 160), drained	2 to 4 pieces, depending on size of eggplant	100 grams
Roasted Red Pepper (page 165), cut into 4 strips about 2 inches long and 1 inch wide	1	20 grams
fresh basil leaves	6 medium	about 3 grams

1. Layer each sandwich with half of the cheese, eggplant, pepper, and basil leaves. Serve immediately.

Panino di Mozzarella • MOZZARELLA SANDWICH
WITH EGGPLANT SPREAD

This is the year-round alternative to the summertime-only Panino di Caprese (page 177). If the star of a Caprese is the tomato, here it's the mozzarella, the mild, milky cheese sparked into life by a dab of intense eggplant spread and a slice of savory Italian ham.

YIELD: 2 sandwiches

INGREDIENTS	MEASURE	WEIGHT
buffalo mozzarella	about six ¼-inch slices	140 grams
Stecca (page 77) or Stirato (page 79), cut in two and split		
Spicy Eggplant Spread (page 166)	about 1 tablespoon	30 grams
prosciutto cotto, sliced as thin as possible	2 slices	about 40 grams

1. Drain the mozzarella in a colander for 1 to 2 hours at room temperature.

2. Slice the cheese about ¼ inch thick.

3. Spread half the eggplant spread on the bottom half of each sandwich, and layer with the mozzarella and prosciutto cotto. Serve immediately.

Panino di Bresaola • DRIED BEEF SANDWICH WITH ARUGULA

Bresaola, air-dried salted beef best savored in near-translucent slices, is beautifully complemented by the light, perky lemon dressing. The bite of the arugula stands up well to the salted beef.

YIELD: 2 sandwiches

INGREDIENTS	MEASURE	WEIGHT
Stecca (page 77) or Stirato (page 79), cut in two and split		
bresaola (see Note), sliced as thin as possible	about 6 slices	60 grams
Lemon Dressing (page 167)	2 tablespoons	28 grams
arugula leaves	about ¼ cup	20 grams
Parmigiano-Reggiano, thinly sliced or in large thin shavings	about ¼ cup	24 grams

1. Layer half the bresaola on the bottom of each sandwich. Drizzle with the dressing and top with the arugula and cheese. Serve immediately.

NOTE: Bresaola is available at Italian food stores and some gourmet markets.

Panino di Barbietola • BEET SANDWICH WITH GOAT CHEESE

This is the rare instance when I turn to a non-Italian cheese for a sandwich, but I find that the tartness of goat cheese is an excellent counterpoint to the earthy sweetness of the beets. I'm sure that's why borscht, the Eastern European beet soup, is so often served with sour cream.

YIELD: 2 sandwiches

INGREDIENTS	MEASURE	WEIGHT
Stecca (page 77) or Stirato (page 79), cut in two and split		
fresh goat cheese, at room temperature (see Note)	2 tablespoons	30 grams
Marinated Beets (page 162), thinly sliced	about 6 slices	110 grams
coarse sea salt	large pinch	
extra virgin olive oil	2 teaspoons	10 grams
arugula leaves	about ¼ cup	20 grams

1. Spread half of the goat cheese on the bottom half of each sandwich. Layer with the beets, sprinkle with the salt, drizzle with the olive oil, and top with the arugula. Serve immediately.

NOTE: There are so many good goat cheeses out there that I don't want to specify a preference: my advice is select a local chèvre from the farmers' market, if you have one. If not, any of the packaged imported goat cheeses that are sold just about everywhere will do.

Panino "PMB" • PANCETTA, MANGO, AND BASIL SANDWICH

The PMB is one of our most popular offerings at the bakery, although the mango must seem unusual to most first-time customers. But I think people get just how fresh it tastes and the beauty of the salty sweetness in the combination.

YIELD: 2 sandwiches

INGREDIENTS	MEASURE	WEIGHT
pancetta sliced thin (2 mm; ask the deli or butcher to slice it for you)	6 slices	60 grams
Stecca (page 77) or Stirato (page 79), cut in two and split		
firm mango, not too soft or sweet, preferably the green Thai variety, peeled and very thinly sliced	1	70 grams
hot red chile powder	2 pinches	
fresh basil leaves	4 large	about 2 grams

1. Preheat the oven to 400 degrees F.

2. Lay the pancetta slices in a single layer on a nonstick or parchment paper–lined baking sheet. Roast until the slices are crisped and the fat is melted, 12 to 16 minutes, depending on how fatty the meat is. Remove from the oven and let cool on a rack, with one end of the pan slightly elevated so the fat drains to the other end.

3. Layer each sandwich with half of the pancetta and sliced mango. Finish with a light sprinkle of chile powder and the basil leaves. Serve immediately.

Panino "PMB."

The "Rampwich" • GREEN ONION BAGNA CAUDA, MOZZARELLA, AND DUCK EGG SANDWICH

What I call the "Rampwich" was put on a pedestal in *New York* magazine, named the sandwich of the week and lavishly praised. But really, I wasn't trying to be all that clever. It was spring. So I was thinking spring ingredients, and the egg and the ramps in my Green Onion Bagna Cauda (page 168), leapt into my mind. (In the bagna cauda recipe I give green onions as the primary ingredient and ramps as a variation, simply because green onions are always available and ramps are not.) A duck egg is a truly nice thing, by the way, a bit more flavorful than a chicken egg. If you use a chicken egg, go for the richest you can find, free-range and organic.

YIELD: 2 sandwiches

EQUIPMENT: An egg harp, also known as an egg slicer, is an excellent tool for this recipe (although a sharp knife will also do). Even if you don't have one, you've probably seen one, a small slicer consisting of many wires. Clamp it down over a hard-boiled egg, and you've got perfect rounds. I also use mine for mozzarella.

INGREDIENTS	MEASURE	WEIGHT
buffalo mozzarella	four ¼-inch slices	55 grams
duck egg (or free-range organic chicken egg)	1	
Stecca (page 77) or Stirato (page 79), cut in two and split		
Green Onion Bagna Cauda (page 168)	about 3 tablespoons	60 grams

1. Drain the mozzarella in a colander for 1 to 2 hours at room temperature.

2. Meanwhile, put the egg in a saucepan with water to cover by about an inch and bring to a boil, then reduce the heat to a simmer and cook for 14 minutes. Fill a bowl with water and ice. When the egg is done, use a slotted spoon to transfer it to the ice water to cool, drain.

3. Peel the egg. Use an egg harp to slice the egg and mozzarella, or cut both by hand about ⅛ inch thick.

4. Layer the sandwiches with the mozzarella and egg and drizzle with the bagna cauda. Serve immediately.

The "Speckeroni" • SPECK WITH PECORINO SANDWICH

The name for this sandwich is drawn from its components, which come together to form a new identity: speck, a smoked Italian ham from northern Italy; tangy sheep's-milk pecorino; and spicy, peppery eggplant spread. The spice is balanced by the savory, smoky meat, mild cheese, and sweet roasted red pepper and paprika, and all the flavors weave together beautifully. (See photo on page 146.)

YIELD: 2 sandwiches

INGREDIENTS	MEASURE	WEIGHT
Spicy Eggplant Spread (page 166)	2 teaspoons	25 grams
Stecca (page 77) or Stirato (page 79), cut in two and split		
aged pecorino Toscano or other pecorino	2 thin slices	about 28 grams
Roasted Red Pepper (page 165), cut into 4 strips about 2 inches long and 1 inch wide	1	20 grams
speck (see headnote), sliced as thin as possible	6 thin slices	60 grams
sweet paprika	2 pinches	

1. Spread half of the eggplant spread on the top half of each sandwich. Layer the bottom halves with the cheese, red pepper, speck, and paprika. Serve immediately.

Panino Frittata • OMELETTE SANDWICH

Normally I make a large number of frittata sandwiches to be sold in the bakery. The most sensible approach for a very big frittata, in my view, is to bake it in a sheet pan and then slice the omelette into rectangles that fit the sandwiches. But when I devised the recipe for the home kitchen I turned to a cast-iron skillet, which distributes heat evenly and is fine for the oven. That, of course, created a round frittata. To make the sandwich neat, you have to trim off the rounded edges and slice the remaining omelette into rectangles that exactly fit the bread. But don't despair about the waste. The trimmings can be refrigerated and saved as snacks. Or they can be cut into smaller pieces to be tossed into a salad, or even placed on crackers as hors d'oeuvres.

YIELD: 2 sandwiches

INGREDIENTS	MEASURE	WEIGHT
Stecca (page 77) or Stirato (page 79), cut in two and split		
Jim's Aioli (page 156)	about 2 tablespoons	60 grams
Frittata Patate (page 170)	1	
Roasted Red Pepper (page 165), cut into 4 strips about 2 inches long and 1 inch wide	1	20 grams
arugula leaves	½ cup	40 grams

1. Spread the aioli on the bottom half of each sandwich.

2. Trim the edges of the frittata to make a rectangle, then cut it in half vertically to shape two pieces that neatly fit the bread.

3. Place a slice of frittata on the bottom half of each sandwich. Layer each with half of the red pepper and then top each with half of the arugula. Close the sandwiches and serve.

Panino Frittata.

Ribollita (page 198).

CHAPTER 6

Stale Bread

If, after making your way through this book, you start doing what I hope you will, which is bake bread all the time because you love doing it, you're going to have a lot of old bread around. It's true that my breads, thanks in part to that long fermentation period, a natural preservative, don't go stale immediately (see "Storing Bread," page 48)—each loaf should be good for at least a couple of days. On the second day, you should still have a slice of bread you don't have to fight to bite into or chew. I call it graceful staling. (You can tell that a lot of today's so-called artisanal breads haven't been well fermented because after a day or two, you can barely make it through the crust and then you hit that stale crumb, dry and hard to swallow.)

Still, if you get bitten by the bread bug, you're going to have some older loaves sitting around. Think like a peasant: this stuff still has value. And your own labor has value too. You don't have to throw the bread away or feed it to the birds. It is still food. You can, of course, grind it into bread crumbs (see page 211) or cut it into croutons for salad or soup. But here are some more inventive recipes to try. Some use bread crumbs as an ingredient, all of them represent a kind of transmutation, where old, dry bread becomes something new. Start with a delicious, if stale, loaf, and a traditional time-tested recipe for using it up, and the results may be a revelation.

Panzanella • BREAD SALAD

This particular bread salad comes from my days in Tuscany in the early 90s. The matron of the place, Alessandra, was a weaver, loom operator, and anarchist. She knew what she was doing in the kitchen. One of the best dishes that routinely showed up on her table was her panzanella. In the preparation, first moisture is restored to dry bread through soaking, then all the excess is vigorously squeezed out, as you would with a sponge, leaving the bread ready to absorb the liquids in the dish. The drier the bread, the longer it will have to soak. (Be a good Italian and do as much of the prep as you can by hand, slicing and ripping directly into the bowl; Alessandra, like many Italians, never uses a cutting board.)

The salad, richly flavorful and filling, gains in crispness and color from a relatively unusual addition, green beans. You can't serve a salad much better than this.

YIELD: 4 servings
EQUIPMENT: A mandoline (optional)

INGREDIENTS	MEASURE	WEIGHT
green beans, trimmed and cut into 1-inch pieces	about 2 loosely packed cups	225 grams
stale, completely dry Basic No-Knead Bread (page 50)	six 1-inch-thick slices	
ripe tomatoes	2 medium	300 grams
red onion	¼ medium	30 grams
roughly chopped capers (optional)	1 teaspoon	4 grams
fresh basil leaves	6 or 7 medium	about 3 grams
extra virgin olive oil	2 tablespoons or to taste	30 grams or to taste
red wine vinegar	1 tablespoon or to taste	15 grams or to taste
table salt	½ teaspoon or to taste	3 grams or to taste
freshly ground black pepper	½ teaspoon or to taste	2 grams or to taste

1. Cook the green beans in a pot of boiling salted water until bright green and just tender but still crisp, about 5 minutes. Drain in a colander, then run under cold water or dunk in an ice water bath until cool; drain well.

2. Put the bread in a medium bowl and cover it with water. Soak until it is saturated, about a minute, then squeeze out as much water as possible. Tear the bread into slightly larger than bite-sized pieces and transfer to a large salad bowl.

3. Cut the tomatoes into chunks, working over the bowl so the bread will catch all of the juices (or chop on a board and add to the bowl, but be sure to collect the juices and add them as well). Use a mandoline to shave the onion into the bowl (or slice as thin as possible and add to the bowl). Add the capers to the bowl, if using. Tear the basil into pieces and add it. Add the green beans.

4. Drizzle the panzanella with the olive oil and vinegar, then sprinkle with the salt and pepper. Toss well, then taste and adjust the seasoning with more vinegar, oil, salt, and/or pepper as necessary. Serve at room temperature, within the hour.

Pappa al Pomodoro • TOMATO BREAD SOUP

This Tuscan classic is really a wonderful garden-fresh sauce that is served as a soup. It's a sauce so pure, so clean and full of flavor, that you can use it on all sorts of things, like gnocchi or linguine. (In fact, the recipe yields an extra cup of sauce; refrigerate it and use in the next day or two for whatever you like.) Here the bread takes the place of pasta, combining with the sauce to create a thick, soulful soup. I've sampled this dish in different Tuscan restaurants and seen it served in small bowls as an appetizer or in large bowls as an entrée. Notice that I specify Pomi brand tomatoes. I like them best for flavor and consistency, and they're widely available; if you can't find them, you can use any Italian chopped tomatoes.

YIELD: 4 to 6 servings

The Pomodoro Sauce (MAKES ABOUT 3 CUPS/360 GRAMS)

INGREDIENTS	MEASURE	WEIGHT
Pomi or other Italian chopped tomatoes	2¼ cups	500 grams
water	2 cups	400 grams
coarsely chopped red onion	⅓ cup	33 grams
peeled and coarsely chopped carrot	½ cup	75 grams
coarsely chopped celery	½ cup	75 grams
extra virgin olive oil	2½ tablespoons	40 grams
fresh basil leaves, torn into pieces	2 medium	about 1 gram
table salt	scant 1 teaspoon or to taste	6 grams or to taste
freshly ground black pepper	⅛ teaspoon or to taste	1 gram or to taste
crushed red pepper flakes	pinch or to taste	

The Soup

INGREDIENTS	MEASURE	WEIGHT
stale white Basic No-Knead Bread (page 50), crusts removed, and cut into 2-inch pieces	about 4 cups	200 grams
Pomodoro Sauce, piping hot (reserve the remaining sauce for another use)	about 2 cups	240 grams
fresh basil leaves	5 medium	about 3 grams

1. To make the sauce, combine all the ingredients in a medium saucepan and bring to a strong simmer over medium heat. Simmer, stirring, until the carrots are tender enough to be crushed with the back of a spoon and the olive oil is bright orange, about 1 hour. Add more water by the tablespoon if the sauce begins to stick to the pan before the carrots are done.

2. Pass the sauce through a food mill, or puree with an immersion blender. Taste and adjust the seasoning with salt and pepper if necessary.

3. To make the soup, put the bread in a large bowl. Pour in the sauce and toss until the bread is coated with sauce but not breaking apart. Tear the basil leaves into pieces and sprinkle over the top. Serve immediately.

Gazpacho

A couple of years ago, I tried an old-fashioned recipe for gazpacho I'd seen in a magazine, and I couldn't stand it: no texture, acidic flavor. So I started fooling around with it. The key, for me, turned out to be the use of some of the staling bread I'd baked a while back to thicken it. Relying on bread as a thickener is not my invention, of course, but I do believe that using extra-flavorful bread like mine makes a difference.

In this recipe, you'll find a term you don't often see in discussions of tomatoes, the "jelly." A tomato has several major components: the fruit wall (the outer shell and the flesh that is part of it), the pith (the lighter-colored core), the seeds, and the jelly, or pulp, that surrounds the seeds. The jelly, with the seeds strained out, is where you find the essence of the fruit, the deep tomato flavor.

YIELD: About 6 cups

INGREDIENTS	MEASURE	WEIGHT
ripe tomatoes	about 4 large	1 kilo
cucumbers	about 2 medium	300 grams
bell pepper (any color), peeled with a vegetable peeler, seeded, and coarsely chopped	1	80 grams
garlic	2 medium cloves	12 grams
torn stale Basic No-Knead Bread (page 50)	¾ cup	40 grams
table salt	1½ teaspoons or to taste	10 grams or to taste
red wine vinegar	1 tablespoon or to taste	15 grams or to taste

1. Place a fine-mesh strainer over a medium bowl. Holding a tomato over the strainer, cut it into quarters. Use a spoon or your fingers to remove the seeds and jelly from the tomato chunks, letting them drop into the strainer. Put the tomato quarters in the bowl. Repeat with the remaining tomatoes. Use the back of the spoon or your fingers to press the tomato jelly through the strainer, extracting as much jelly from the seeds as possible. Discard the seeds.

2. Peel the cucumbers, halve lengthwise, and use a spoon to remove their seeds. Coarsely chop.

3. In a blender, combine the tomato flesh and jelly, the cucumbers, and the bell pepper with the remaining ingredients, in batches if necessary, and pulse for a couple of seconds at a time (about 10 to 15 times) until the mixture is very finely chopped but not pureed.

4. Taste the gazpacho and add more salt and vinegar if you think it needs it. Serve at room temperature, or chill for up to 2 hours before serving (if you serve the gazpacho cold, it may require a bit more salt).

Ribollita • THICK TUSCAN BEAN AND KALE SOUP

The name of this Tuscan soup literally means "reboiled." It's usually cooked and allowed to stand for a period of time—it varies depending on the cook—before being reheated. The process softens the vegetables and allows the flavors to develop. Tomatoes are my untraditional addition—I like the acidity they contribute. For more flavor, I sometimes throw a piece of Parmesan cheese rind and/or a bit of chopped pancetta in with the beans. The soup doesn't really require any embellishment; even the traditional drizzle of good olive oil and a sprinkle of Parmigiano-Reggiano should be considered optional garnishes. Once you've tried the recipe as written, you can adjust the amount of bread to your taste—some people prefer it soupy, others like it with almost all the liquid absorbed. (See photo on p. 188.)

YIELD: 6 to 8 servings

INGREDIENTS	MEASURE	WEIGHT
dried romano (borlotti) beans	about ½ cup	75 grams
extra virgin olive oil	2 tablespoons	30 grams
coarsely chopped red onion	1 cup	100 grams
peeled and coarsely chopped carrot	½ cup	75 grams
coarsely chopped celery	½ cup	75 grams
dried bay leaves	2 small	
table salt	2 teaspoons or to taste	16 grams or to taste
crushed red pepper flakes	1 teaspoon or to taste	2 grams or to taste
Savoy cabbage, cored and thinly sliced	7 cups	300 grams
cavolo nero (aka dinosaur, Tuscan, black, or lacinato kale) or green kale, stems removed, leaves thinly sliced	about ½ bunch	150 grams
diced tomatoes in juice, drained, juice reserved, and chopped	one 14½-ounce can	411 grams
water	5½ cups	1.25 kilos
Parmigiano-Reggiano cheese rind (optional)	2 to 4 tablespoons	30 to 60 grams
very stale Basic No-Knead Bread (page 50), torn or cut into 1-inch cubes	1½ cups	80 grams
extra virgin olive oil for drizzling (optional)		
shaved or grated Parmigiano-Reggiano for serving (optional)		

1. Rinse and drain the beans. Place them in a medium bowl, cover with plenty of cool water, and soak for 8 hours.

2. In a large heavy pot, heat the olive oil over medium-low heat. Add the onion, carrot, celery, bay leaves, half the salt, and the red pepper, stir, and cook covered, stirring occasionally, until the onions are semitranslucent and just starting to brown on the edges, about 9 minutes.

3. Add the cabbage and kale, cover, and cook, stirring occasionally, until wilted, about 15 minutes.

4. Drain the soaked beans and add to the pot. Add the water, tomatoes and their juice, and cheese rind, if using, and bring to a boil, then reduce to a simmer and cook until the beans are tender and the vegetables are very soft, 2 to 3 hours. (The soup can be cooled and refrigerated at this point. Reheat over medium heat before adding the bread.) Discard the cheese rind.

5. Meanwhile, if the bread is not completely brittle, spread it on a baking sheet and toast in the oven at 250 degrees F until it crumbles at your touch.

6. Add the bread to the soup, folding it in gently so as not to break it up too much. Let the bread soften and absorb the liquid for a few minutes, then taste and adjust the seasoning with salt and or red pepper flakes as necessary.

7. Ladle the soup into the bowls. Drizzle with olive oil and sprinkle with grated cheese if desired, and serve immediately.

Tomato Bruschetta

And God created great tomatoes. If there is anything more wonderful than an absolutely perfectly ripe tomato, you'll have to let me know. When the season is right and the tomato is everything it can be, sometimes all you want to do is slice it and savor it. But there are recipes, like this bruschetta, that actually add to an already perfect food. Basically it's tomato, olive oil, and terrific garlic-rubbed toast (without the tomato, bruschetta is simply garlic bread), perhaps with a bit of additional seasoning. As simple as it is, it is possible to ruin a tomato bruschetta, as too many restaurants do, by failing to keep in mind that you are engaged in an exercise in perfection. It's all about quality. In this recipe, I present the most basic approach, using toasted slices of a loaf of the basic no-knead bread baked yesterday or two days ago. Notice that the salt on the tomatoes comes late in the process. If you add the salt too early, the bruschetta will be watery. Always exercise restraint in embellishing bruschetta. And when you cut the tomato, dear friend, be gentle.

YIELD: 6 servings

INGREDIENTS	MEASURE	WEIGHT
perfectly ripe heirloom tomato (see headnote)	1 large	about 200 grams
extra virgin olive oil	¼ cup	60 grams
day-old Basic No-Knead Bread (page 50)	six ½-inch-thick slices	
garlic	2 medium cloves	12 grams
crushed red pepper flakes (optional)	large pinch	
table salt	about ¼ teaspoon or to taste	2 grams or to taste
fresh basil leaves (optional)	3 large	about 2 grams

1. Core the tomato. Use a serrated knife to cut the tomato into ½-inch-thick slices and then into ½-inch cubes, saving as much of the juices on the cutting board as possible. Put the tomato and its juices in a bowl and add the olive oil. (Do not be tempted to salt at this point.)

2. Toast the bread until it is crunchy on both sides but not brown. Rub the surface of one side of the warm bread slices with the garlic cloves (the toasted bread will slightly grate the garlic) and sprinkle with a bit of red pepper, if using. Top each slice of bread with some of the tomatoes, sprinkle with a tiny pinch of the salt, and garnish with the torn basil leaves if you like. Serve immediately.

VARIATION · NEAPOLITAN TOMATO BRUSCHETTA

Add 4 or 5 torn fresh oregano leaves or a large pinch of dried Italian oregano to the tomatoes. Grate a small clove of garlic into the mix as well. Proceed as directed, leaving out the basil.

Roasted Red Pepper Bruschetta

This is a somewhat different bruschetta than the traditional tomato one that precedes it. During a photo session for this book, hunger struck everybody in the room and I reached for what I had in the kitchen. There were no tomatoes, so I switched to roasted red peppers. I didn't need to add salt because I was going to use salty capers and anchovies. It worked out so well that when I opened my Manhattan resturant Co., I decided to serve this bruschetta in small, easy to handle portions, cutting the slices of bread into quarters, rather than using the slices whole. When you plan to prepare this version try to think ahead and save a couple of the larger slices from the loaf so that the quarters won't be too small.

YIELD: 8 hors d'oeuvres

INGREDIENTS	MEASURE	WEIGHT
Roasted Red Peppers (page 165), cut into strips about 1 inch long and ½ inch wide	1¼ cups	200 grams
oil-packed anchovies, coarsely chopped	1 tablespoon	15 grams
salted capers	2 teaspoons	10 grams
red wine vinegar	1 teaspoon	4 grams
stale Basic No-Knead Bread (page 50)	two ½- to 1-inch-thick slices	
garlic, peeled	1 medium clove	6 grams

1. In a medium bowl, combine the red peppers, anchovies, capers, and red wine vinegar.

2. Toast the bread until it is crunchy on both sides but not brown. Rub the surface of one side of each of the warm bread slices with the garlic (the toasted bread will slightly grate the garlic). Cut both slices of bread into quarters.

3. Top the bread generously with the red pepper mixture, about 40 grams or about 2 tablespoons for each quarter. Serve immediately.

Roasted Red Pepper Bruschetta.

Budino • BREAD PUDDING TART

I suspect you've eaten bread pudding before, and, if you're like untold millions, you have a great affection for this soft, creamy, vanilla-accented comfort food. This version has a little something extra going for it. When I came up with it, I was thinking about the classic tarte Tatin, the French upside-down apple tarte topped with caramel. When unmolded, this dessert has its crust on the bottom (the traditional and very simple buttery Italian *pasta frolla*) and caramel on the top. In between is the budino, a fruity bread pudding. Read the recipe through before you get started so you have a sense of the timing: this isn't an instant pudding, but it may be a timeless one.

YIELD: One 12-inch tart
EQUIPMENT: An electric mixer fitted with a paddle attachment or a hand mixer; a 12-inch tart pan or a heavy 12-inch ovenproof skillet

Budino Filling

INGREDIENTS	MEASURE	WEIGHT
eggs	3 large	about 180 grams
heavy cream	2 cups	450 grams
whole milk	¾ cup	180 grams
sugar	½ cup	95 grams
vanilla extract	¾ teaspoon	5 grams
stale Basic No-Knead Bread (page 50), cut into 2-inch pieces	about 3¼ cups	175 grams

Pasta Frolla (TART CRUST)

INGREDIENTS	MEASURE	WEIGHT
bread flour	1½ cups	210 grams
table salt	pinch	1 gram
unsalted butter, softened	8 tablespoons (1 stick)	115 grams
sugar	¼ cup	48 grams
egg	1 large	about 60 grams

Caramel

INGREDIENTS	MEASURE	WEIGHT
sugar	¾ cup plus 1 tablespoon	155 grams
unsalted butter	½ tablespoon	7 grams

Fruit

INGREDIENTS	MEASURE	WEIGHT
peaches or nectarines (see Note)	2 medium	400 grams

1. To make the filling, lightly beat the eggs in a medium bowl; set aside. In a small pot, combine the cream, milk, and sugar and bring to a simmer over medium heat, stirring until the sugar is dissolved. Slowly pour about half of the hot cream mixture into the eggs, whisking constantly, then whisk in the rest. Stir in the vanilla extract.

2. Put the bread in a wide shallow dish or bowl. Add the egg mixture and stir to coat the bread. Let cool for 5 to 10 minutes, then cover and refrigerate until the bread has soaked up nearly all of the egg mixture, at least 6 hours. (The mixture can be refrigerated for up to 3 days.)

3. To make the pasta frolla, in a small bowl, whisk together the flour and salt. Put the butter and sugar in the bowl of an electric mixer fitted with the paddle attachment and beat on high speed until the butter is light and fluffy and the sugar is dissolved, 2 to 3 minutes. Add the egg and beat on medium speed until incorporated. Stir in the flour just until incorporated. Scrape the dough onto a piece of plastic wrap, shape it into a disk, and wrap well. Refrigerate until firm but not rock hard, at least 30 minutes.

4. Meanwhile make the caramel: Cook the sugar in a skillet over medium-high heat, swirling the pan until the sugar is melted into an amber caramel, about 5 minutes. Add the butter, tipping and swirling the pan until the butter has melted and smoothly blended (emulsified) with the caramel. Set aside to cool slightly, then coat the bottom of the tart pan, if using.

RECIPE CONTINUES ON NEXT PAGE

5. Lightly dust a work surface with flour and roll out the tart dough to a 12-inch round, about ⅛ inch thick. Set aside on a piece of wax or parchment paper and refrigerate for half an hour, or until needed.

6. To bake the tart, preheat the oven to 400 degrees F.

7. With a vegetable peeler, peel 1 of the peaches or nectarines and cut it into approximately 1-inch cubes. Stir the fruit into the bread and custard mixture until evenly distributed. Slice the other peach or nectarine (no need to peel) into thin wedges and arrange the pieces decoratively in the caramel-lined tart pan or ovenproof skillet. Spread the filling mixture evenly in the pan or skillet. Lay the tart crust over the filling and use the tip of a paring knife to trim the edges of the dough to just inside the rim of the pan or skillet (you don't want it adhering to the rim).

8. Place the budino on a parchment- or foil-lined baking sheet (in case it bubbles over during baking). Bake until the crust is a deep golden brown and the caramel is bubbling up at the sides, about 45 minutes. Remove from the oven and immediately run the tip of a paring knife around the edge of the pan or skillet to help loosen it. Using pot holders or oven mitts, invert a serving plate over the budino and very carefully flip the pan or skillet over (protect your hands and wrists, as some very hot caramel can run out). Leave the pan or skillet on top of the inverted tart until it is cool enough to handle.

9. Gently remove the pan or skillet. If any of the slices of fruit stick to the pan or skillet, use a spatula or knife to carefully scrape them off, and replace them on the tart. Serve the budino warm or at room temperature. It can be stored at room temperature for up to 2 days or in the refrigerator for up to 4 days.

NOTE: Feel free to substitute other fruits for the nectarines or peaches—apricots, plums, cherries, banana, apple, whatever is the best at the moment.

BRUNA'S PASTA FROLLA

During the time I baked for Joe Allen's restaurants (see page 27), he sent me to Italy to stay in his rustic getaway, a stone house in the middle of a chestnut forest just outside San Casicano de Bagni, not far from Rome. I was there to relax and to soak up the baking culture of the town. *Bagni*, by the way, refers to the stone-fenced thermal baths in the woods, where I used to bathe naked, as everybody else did back then. I honed in on the Boni family, who owned a pizzeria called Bar Centrale (Joe opened a place with the same name in New York), with a little kitchen where a lot of baking skill resided. The matriarch of the family was named Bruna, and on a recent trip back, I recognized her immediately, standing outside in her green dress, wearing sneakers to ease the burden of using her walker.

I owe Bruna a debt of gratitude for teaching me, if somewhat unwillingly, how to bake the Italian tarts called *crostate*. I return to her *pasta frolla*, the sweet crust that is the foundation of a great many desserts, again and again, in recipes like my Budino (page 204). In baking, I always strive to create something—like my basic bread dough—so fundamental that it can play multiple roles, so I consider a dough as versatile as pasta frolla to be a feather in any baker's cap. Fortunately the recipe is forgiving, with many variations, because Bruna didn't make my job as easy as she might have.

"Flour," she'd say, "eggs, sugar—you're smart. Figure it out." Her caginess meant I never pinned down her measurements, but I learned a lot just from watching her handle the ingredients: she wasn't overly precise or gentle, but her assurance meant that she worked quickly and didn't overwork the dough. And I learned at least as much simply by eating every variety of pie, tart, and cookie that she turned out of the pizza ovens. What you're looking for in the perfect pasta frolla is a pleasantly crumbly crust that's not too buttery and only moderately sweet. It should be sturdy enough to hold up to many a dessert, but never tough. The formula took some playing around with back home, but I did figure it out. I save you the guesswork (see pages 204 and 205).

Tortino di Cioccolato.

Tortino di Cioccolato • CHOCOLATE TORTE

This chocolatey torte makes terrific use of dry bread crumbs to add texture and body. I like to make the tortes in cupcake molds. (As I write this, we've been in sort of a cupcake-crazy period in New York.) It's possible to prepare the torte in a larger mold, but because it has a delicate, fragile crumb, it can be a bit difficult to slice neatly. So I prefer the cupcake size.

YIELD: 12 individual tortes

EQUIPMENT: A stand mixer fitted with the whisk attachment or a hand mixer, a muffin pan with 12 (⅓- to ½-cup) cups, and 12 paper cupcake liners

INGREDIENTS	MEASURE	WEIGHT
unsalted butter	8 tablespoons (1 stick)	115 grams
semisweet chocolate, roughly chopped	4 ounces	115 grams
sugar	1 cup plus 1 tablespoon	202 grams
eggs, separated	4 large	about 240 grams
fine dry Homemade Bread Crumbs (page 211)	¼ cup	40 grams
table salt	pinch	1 gram

1. Preheat the oven to 400 degrees F.

2. In a small saucepan over low heat (or in a bowl in the microwave), melt the butter. Combine the chocolate with ⅔ cup plus 1 tablespoon of the sugar in a medium bowl, add the hot melted butter, and stir a few times. Let sit for 3 or 4 minutes to melt the chocolate, then stir until smooth.

3. Put the egg yolks in a large bowl and slowly whisk in the chocolate mixture until thoroughly combined. Mix in the bread crumbs very thoroughly.

RECIPE CONTINUES ON NEXT PAGE

4. Put the egg whites and salt in the bowl of an electric mixer fitted with the whisk attachment, or in a medium bowl if you're using a hand mixer. Whip at medium speed until the whites are foamy, then reduce the speed to medium-low and gradually add the remaining ⅓ cup sugar. Raise the speed to medium and continue whipping until the whites form stiff, shiny peaks (if they become dry or clumpy, they're overwhipped and will not give the torte the light, smooth texture it needs; dump them and start over with new egg whites). Use a rubber spatula or whisk to fold a large scoop of the meringue into the chocolate mixture until incorporated (this will lighten it), then gently fold in the remaining meringue.

5. Line 12 muffin cups with paper liners. Fill each cup approximately three-quarters full. Bake the tortini for about 10 minutes, until they are puffed up and just set in the middle. Remove from the oven and cool completely on a rack. The tortini will keep in an airtight container at room temperature for up to 3 days.

Homemade Bread Crumbs

I like to prepare bread crumbs by starting with what are essentially croutons. Cutting the bread slices into cubes hastens the drying and also facilitates the work of the food processor. Of course, if you want to stop at the crouton stage, be my guest and use the toasted cubes to garnish soup or salads. A loaf of my bread yields about 6 cups of bread crumbs. If you want less, use just part of a loaf. Or make the full amount: the bread crumbs keep well for several weeks if you store them in a cool, dark place.

YIELD: About 6 cups

INGREDIENTS	MEASURE	WEIGHT
day-old Basic No-Knead Bread (page 50)	1 loaf	

1. Slice the loaf of bread into ¾-inch slices, then cut the slices into ¾-inch cubes. Place the cubes on a baking sheet and allow to dry overnight, or for at least 12 hours.

2. Preheat the oven to 400 degrees F.

3. Toast the bread cubes in the oven for 8 minutes. Allow to cool.

4. Pulse the crumbs in a food processor to the desired coarseness, at least 2 minutes.

Index

Note: Page numbers in *italics* indicate pictures; page numbers in **boldface** refer to recipes themselves.

A

All-Clad loaf pans, 105
all-purpose flour, 48
almond(s)
    Almond-Apricot Bread, **108-9**
    Fennel-Raisin Bread, **112-13,** 140
    Focaccia Dolce, **144-45**
    Sweet Focaccia, **144-45**
Almond-Apricot Bread, **108-9**
almond butter
    Almond-Apricot Bread, **108-9**
Amy's Bread (bakery), 27
anchovies
    Green Onion, Anchovy, and Garlic Sauce, **168-69**
    Green Onion Bagna Cauda, **168-69**
    Lemon Dressing, **167**
    Roasted Red Pepper Bruschetta, **202,** *203*
anise-flavored liqueur
    Fennel-Raisin Bread, **112-13**
Apple Bread, **99-100**
apricot(s)
    Almond-Apricot Bread, **108-9**
    Focaccia Dolce, **144-45**
    Sweet Focaccia, **144-45**
apricot jam
    Focaccia Dolce, **144-45**
    Sweet Focaccia, **144-45**
artichoke(s)
    Artichoke and Ham Sandwich, 160, **176**
    Artichoke Confit, **159-60,** 176
    Panino di Carciofi e Prosciutto Cotto, 160, **176**
Artichoke and Ham Sandwich, 160, **176**
Artichoke Confit, **159-60,** 176
arugula
    Beet Sandwich with Goat Cheese, 163, **181**
    Dried Beef Sandwich with Arugula, 167, **180**

Omelette Sandwich, 171, **186,** *187*
Panino di Barbietola, 163, **181**
Panino di Bresaola, 167, **180**
Panino di Manzo, 151, 156, 164, **173**
Panino Frittata, 171, **186,** *187*
Roast Beef Sandwich with Aioli, 151, 156, *163,* 164, **173**
Asiago cheese
    Cheese Bread, **71-72,** *72*
    Pane con Formaggio, **71-72,** *72*

B

bacteria, naturally occurring, 40
baguettes
    Italian Baguette, **79-80**
    Stecca, *56, 76,* **77-78,** *77,* 172, 173, 174, 176, 177, 178, 179, 180, 181, 182, 184, 186
    Stecca Pomodori, All'Olive, O Al'Aglio, **78**
    Stick or Small Baguette, *56, 76,* **77-78,** 172, 173, 174, 176, 177, 178, 179, 180, 181, 182, 184, 186
    Stirato, **79-80,** 172, 173, 174, 175, 176, 177, 178, 179, 180, 181, 182, 184, 185, 186
baking bread, 41-42, 51
baking sheets, *44*
Banana Leaf Rolls, **87-88,** *89*
Basic No-Knead Bread, 30, **50-52,** *53-55,* 58, 192, 195, 196, 198, 200, 202, 204, 211
Basic Pizza Dough, **117-18,** *119,* 120, 126, 128, 129, 132, 133, 134, 136
basil
    Bread Salad, **192-93**
    Eggplant Sandwich with Roasted Red Pepper, 161, 165, **178**

basil (*continued*)

    Mozzarella and Tomato Sandwich, **177,** 179

    Pancetta, Mango, and Basil Sandwich, 149, **182,** *183*

    Panino di Caprese, **177,** 179

    Panino di Melanzane, 149, 161, 165, **178**

    Panino "PMB," 149, **182,** *183*

    Panzanella, **192-93**

    Tomato Bruschetta, **200-201**

beans. *See* borlotti beans; green beans; romano beans

beef

    Dried Beef Sandwich with Arugula, 167, **180**

    Panino di Bresaola, 167, **180**

    Panino di Manzo, 151, 156, *163,* 164, **173**

    Roast Beef Sandwich with Aioli, 151, 156, *163,* 164, **173**

    Rosemary Roast Beef, 149, **150-51,** 173

beer as ingredient, 92

beets

    Beet Sandwich with Goat Cheese, 163, **181**

    Marinated Beets, **163-64**

    Panino di Barbietola, 163, **181**

Beet Sandwich with Goat Cheese, 163, **181**

bell peppers

    Eggplant Sandwich with Roasted Red Pepper, 161, 165, **178**

    Gazpacho, **196-97**

    Omelette Sandwich, 171, **186,** *187*

    Panino di Melanzane, 149, 161, 165, **178**

    Panino Frittata, 171, **186,** *187*

    Roasted Red Pepper Bruschetta, **202,** *203*

    Roasted Red Peppers, **165**

Benriner mandolines, 125

Bittman, Mark, 39

borlotti beans

    Ribollita, *188,* **198-99**

    Thick Tuscan Bean and Kale Soup, *188,* **198-99**

bowls, *44*

box graters, *123*

bread

    baking, 41-42, 51

    no-knead technique for making. *See* no-knead technique

    slicing, 42, 47

    storing, 49

bread crumbs

    Homemade Bread Crumbs, 132, 209, **211**

bread flour, 48

Bread Pudding Tart, **204-6**

Bread Salad, **192-93**

bresaola

    Dried Beef Sandwich with Arugula, 167, **180**

    Panino di Bresaola, 167, **180**

Bron mandolines, 125

bruschetta

    Neapolitan Tomato Bruschetta, **201**

    Roasted Red Pepper Bruschetta, **202,** *203*

    Tomato Bruschetta, **200-201**

brushes, *44, 124*

Budino, **204-6,** *207*

buffalo mozzarella

    Green Onion Bagna Cauda, Mozzarella, and Duck Egg Sandwich, **184-85**

    Mozzarella and Tomato Sandwich, **177**

    Mozzarella Sandwich with Eggplant Spread, 166, **179**

    Panino di Caprese, **177,** 179

    Panino di Mozzarella, 166, **179**

    "Rampwich," 169, **184-85**

buttermilk

    Irish Brown Bread with Currants, **94**

    Jim's Irish Brown Bread, **93-94,** *95*

C

cabbage. *See* Savoy cabbage

caramelization, 41

carbon dioxide bubbles, rising of dough and, 41

Carrot Bread, *96,* **97-98**

cast-iron pots, 45

cauliflower

    Cauliflower Pizza, **128-29**

    Pizza Cavolfiore, **128-29**

celery root

    Celery Root Pizza, **133**

    Pizza Radici di Sedano, **133**

cheese. *See also* Asiago cheese; buffalo mozzarella; Crucolo cheese; Fontina cheese; goat cheese; Grana Padano cheese; Gruyère cheese; mozzarella

cheese; Parmigiano-Reggiano cheese;
pecorino cheese; Swiss cheese
Cheese Bread, **71-72,** *72*
Pane con Formaggio, **71-72,** *72*
saltiness of, *72*
Cheese Bread, **71-72,** *72*
cherries
Focaccia Dolce, **144-45**
Sweet Focaccia, **144-45**
chocolate
Chocolate Torte, *208,* **209-10**
Coconut-Chocolate Bread, *84,* **85-86**
Tortino di Cioccolato, *208,* **209-10**
Ciabatta, **81-82,** *83*
Citrus Roast Pork, **152-53,** *153, 155,* 174
clay bakers, 79, 80, 81, *83*
coconut
Banana Leaf Rolls, **87-88,** *89*
Coconut-Chocolate Bread, *84,* **85-86**
cold weather, effect on rising time, 51
cooling bread, 42, 47, 51
cooling racks, *44, 124*
corn
Fresh Corn Bread, **110-11**
cornmeal
Fresh Corn Bread, **110-11**
cream
Bread Pudding Tart, **204-6**
Budino, **204-6,** 207
Crucolo cheese
Artichoke and Ham Sandwich, 160, **176**
Panino di Carciofi e Prosciutto Cotto, 160, **176**
Cuban Sandwich, 153, 156, 157, 158, **174,** *175*
cucumbers
Gazpacho, **196-97**
Homemade Pickles, **157,** 174
currants
Carrot Bread, *96,* **97-98**
Irish Brown Bread with Currants, **94**

D

dates
Banana Leaf Rolls, **87-88,** *89*
Focaccia Dolce, **144-45**
Sweet Focaccia, **144-45**

desserts
Bread Pudding Tart, **204-6**
Budino, **204-6,** 207
Chocolate Torte, *208,* **209-10**
Tortino di Cioccolato, *208,* **209-10**
dough, rising of, 41, 50-51
dough cutters, *43*
dressing
Lemon Dressing, **167**
dried apricots
Almond-Apricot Bread, **108-9**
Dried Beef Sandwich with Arugula, *163,* 167,
180
dried cherries
Focaccia Dolce, **144-45**
Sweet Focaccia, **144-45**
duck eggs
Green Onion Bagna Cauda, Mozzarella, and
Duck Egg Sandwich, **184-85**
"Rampwich," 169, **184-85**

E

egg(s)
Bread Pudding Tart, **204-6**
Budino, **204-6,** 207
Chocolate Torte, *208,* **209-10**
Frittata Patate, **170-71,** 186
Green Onion Bagna Cauda, Mozzarella, and
Duck Egg Sandwich, **184-85**
Omelette Sandwich, 171, **186,** *187*
Panino Frittata, 171, **186,** 187
Potato Omelette, **170-71**
"Rampwich," 169, **184-85**
Tortino di Cioccolato, *208,* **209-10**
eggplant
Eggplant Sandwich with Roasted Red
Pepper, 161, 165, **178**
Marinated Eggplant, **160-61,** 166
Mozzarella Sandwich with Eggplant Spread,
166, **179**
Panino di Melanzane, 149, 161, 165, **178**
Panino di Mozzarella, 166, **179**
Spicy Eggplant Spread, **166,** 179, 185
Eggplant Sandwich with Roasted Red Pepper,
161, 165, **178**

egg slicer, 184
Emile Henry pots, 45
equipment
    baking sheets, *44*
    bowls, *44*
    box graters, *123*
    brushes, *44, 124*
    cooling racks, *44, 124*
    dough cutters, *43*
    egg slicer, 184
    Foley food mills, *124*
    knives, *43*, 122, *123, 124*, 125
    mandolines, *124*, 125
    measuring cups, *43, 44*
    measuring spoons, *43*
    mezzalunas, 122, *123*
    peels, *123*
    pie plates, *123*
    pizza cutters, *124*
    for pizzas, 122, *123, 124*, 125
    pizza stones, *123*
    pizza wheels, 122
    plastic spatulas, *123*
    pots, 42, 45
    protective gloves, 125
    rubber spatulas, *43*
    scales, *43*
    tea towels, *44*
    timer, *44*
    wooden spoons, *43, 124*

F

fennel
    Fennel Pizza, **140**
    Fennel-Raisin Bread, **112-13,** 140
    Pizza Finocchio, **140**
Fennel Pizza, **140**
Fennel-Raisin Bread, **112-13,** 140
fermentation, long, 39-41, 50-51
flour, 39, 49, 61
Focaccia, **141-42,** *143*
Focaccia Dolce, **144-45**
Foley food mills, *124*
Fontina cheese
    Cheese Bread, **71-72,** *72*

Pane con Formaggio, **71-72,** *72*
Forno a Legna da Sergio, 30
Forno Campo de Fiori, 28-29
freezing pizza dough, 117
Fresh Corn Bread, **110-11**
Frittata Patate, **170-71,** 186
fruit. *See specific fruits*
fruit jam
    Focaccia Dolce, **144-45**
    Peanut Butter and Jelly Bread, *103, 104,*
        105-6, *107*
    Sweet Focaccia, **144-45**

G

garlic
    Stecca Pomodori, All'Olive, O Al'Aglio, **78**
    Stecca with Tomatoes, Olives, or Garlic, **78**
Gazpacho, **196-97**
gloves, protective, 125
gluten, 39-40
    protein content of flour and, 48
    rising of dough and, 41
goat cheese
    Beet Sandwich with Goat Cheese, 163, **181**
    Panino di Barbietola, 163, **181**
Grana Padano cheese
    Fennel Pizza, **140**
    Pizza Cavolfiore, **128-29**
    Pizza Finocchio, **140**
Grandaisy, 33
grapes
    Schicciata D'Uva, **139**
    Sweet Raisin and Grape Pizza, **139**
graters, *123*
green beans
    Bread Salad, **192-93**
    Panzanella, **192-93**
green olives. *See olive(s)*
Green Onion, Anchovy, and Garlic Sauce,
    168-69
Green Onion Bagna Cauda, **168-69,** 184
Green Onion Bagna Cauda, Mozzarella, and
    Duck Egg Sandwich, 169, **184-85**
green Sicilian colossal olives, 70
Gruyère cheese

Cuban Sandwich, 153, 156, 157, 158, **174,** *175*
Panino Cubano, 153, 156, 157, 158, **174,** *175*
Pizza Zucchine, **132**
Zucchini Pizza, **132**
Guiness stout
    Irish Brown Bread with Currants, **94**
    Jim's Irish Brown Bread, **93-94,** *95*

H

ham. *See* pancetta; prosciutto cotto; prosciutto
    di Parma; speck
Homemade Bread Crumbs, 132, 209, **211**
Homemade Pickles, **157,** 174
Homemade Spicy Mustard, **158,** 174

I

IGP *(Indicazione Geografica Protetta),* 30
ingredients. *See also specific ingredients*
    slicing, 12, 122, 125
    weighing, 48
Irish Brown Bread with Currants, **94**
Italian Baguette, **79-80**

J

Jim's Aioli, **156,** 173, 174, 186
Jim's Irish Brown Bread, **93-94,** *95*
Jones Beach Bread, **90-91**
juices as ingredient, 92

K

kalamata olives, 70
kale
    Ribollita, *188,* **198-99**
    Thick Tuscan Bean and Kale Soup, *188,*
        198-99
knives, *43,* 122, *123, 124*
Kyocera mandolines, 125

L

Le Creuset pots, 45
lemons and lemon juice
    Artichoke Confit, **159-60,** 176
    Lemon Dressing, **167**
lemon zest
    Citrus Roast Pork, **152-53,** *153, 155,* 174
loaf pans, 105
Lodge pots, 45

M

Maillard reaction, 41
mandolines, *124,* 125
mangoes
    Pancetta, Mango, and Basil Sandwich, 149,
        182, *183*
    Panino "PMB," 149, **182,** *183*
Marinated Beets, **163-64**
Marinated Eggplant, **160-61,** 166
Marinated Sun-Dried Tomatoes, **164,** 166, 173
McGee, Harold, 39-40
measuring cups, *43, 44*
measuring ingredients, 48
measuring spoons, *43*
mezzalunas, 122, *123*
milk
    Bread Pudding Tart, **204-6**
    Budino, **204-6,** 207
mozzarella cheese. *See also* buffalo mozzarella
    Mozzarella and Tomato Sandwich, **177,** 179
    Mozzarella Sandwich with Eggplant Spread,
        166, **179**
    Panino di Caprese, **177,** 179
    Panino di Mozzarella, 166, **179**
mushrooms
    Mushroom Pizza, **126,** *127*
    Pizza Funghi, **126,** 127, 128

N

Neapolitan Tomato Bruschetta, **201**
nectarines
    Bread Pudding Tart, **204-6**

nectarines (*continued*)
    Budino, **204-6,** 207
no-knead technique, 37-48
    evolution of, 34-35
    flour and, 39, 48
    heat and, 41-42
    pots for, 42, 45
    salt and, 41
    slow fermentation and, 39-41
    yeast and, 40-41
nori
    Ocean Bread with Nori, **91**

O

Ocean Bread with Nori, **91**
olive(s)
    Cauliflower Pizza, **128-29**
    Olive Bread, 68, **69-70**
    Pane all'Olive, 68, **69-70**
    Pizza Cavolfiore, **128-29**
    Stecca Pomodori, All'Olive, O Al'Aglio, **78**
    Stecca with Tomatoes, Olives, or Garlic, **78**
    types of, 70
Olive Bread, 68, **69-70**
omelette
    Frittata Patate, **170-71,** 186
    Omelette Sandwich, 171, **186,** 187
    Panino Frittata, 171, **186,** 187
    Potato Omelette, **170-71**
Omelette Sandwich, 171, **186,** 187
On Food and Cooking (McGee), 39
onion(s)
    Bread Salad, **192-93**
    Celery Root Pizza, **133**
    Gazpacho, **196-97**
    Marinated Beets, **163-64**
    Mushroom Pizza, **126,** 127
    Onion Pizza, **134,** 135
    Panzanella, **192-93**
    Pizza Cipolla, **134,** 135
    Pizza Funghi, **126,** 127, 128
    Pizza Patate, **129-30,** *131*
    Pizza Radici di Sedano, **133**
    Potato Pizza, **129-30,** *131*
    Ribollita, *188,* **198-99**

Thick Tuscan Bean and Kale Soup, *188,* **198-99**
    Tomato Pizza with Pancetta and Onion, **121**
Onion Pizza, **134,** 135
oregano
    Neapolitan Tomato Bruschetta, **201**
Orso, 27-28
"oven spring," 41
oven temperature, 42

P

pancetta
    Pancetta, Mango, and Basil Sandwich, 149, **182,** *183*
    Pancetta Bread, **73-74**
    Pancetta Rolls, **74,** *75*
    Panino "PMB," 149, **182,** *183*
    Tomato Pizza with Pancetta and Onion, **121**
Pancetta, Mango, and Basil Sandwich, 149, **182,** *183*
Pancetta Bread, **73-74**
Pancetta Rolls, **74,** *75*
Pan co' Santi, **66-67,** *67*
Pane all'Olive, *68,* **69-70**
Pane con Formaggio, **71-72,** *72*
Pane Integrale, *60,* **61-62**
panini. *See* sandwiches; sandwich ingredients
Panino Cubano, 153, 156, 157, 158, **174,** *175*
Panino de Barbietola, 163, **181**
Panino di Bresaola, *163,* 167, **180**
Panino di Caprese, **177,** 179
Panino di Carciofi e Prosciutto Cotto, 160, **176**
Panino di Manzo, 151, 156, *163,* 164, **173**
Panino di Melanzane, 149, 161, 165, **178**
Panino di Mozzarella, 166, **179**
Panino Frittata, 171, **186,** *187*
Panino "PMB," 149, **182,** *183*
Panzanella, **192-93**
Pappa al Pomodoro, **194-95**
Parmigiano-Reggiano cheese
    Cauliflower Pizza, **128-29**
    Dried Beef Sandwich with Arugula, 167, **180**
    Fennel Pizza, **140**
    Panino di Bresaola, 167, **180**

Pizza Cavolfiore, **128-29**
Pizza Finocchio, **140**
Ribollita, *188*, **198-99**
Thick Tuscan Bean and Kale Soup, *188*,
    198-99
pasta frolla, 204, 205, 207
peaches
    Bread Pudding Tart, **204-6**
    Budino, **204-6,** 207
Peanut Bread, **101-2**
Peanut Butter and Jelly Bread, *103, 104,* **105-6,**
    107
pecorino cheese
    Cheese Bread, **71-72,** *72*
    Eggplant Sandwich with Roasted Red
        Pepper, 161, 165, **178**
    Pane con Formaggio, **71-72,** *72*
    Panino di Melanzane, 149, 161, 165, **178**
    "Speckeroni," *146,* 164, 166, **185**
    Speck with Pecorino Sandwich, *146,* 164, 166,
        185
peels, *123*
pickles
    Cuban Sandwich, 153, 156, 157, 158, **174,** *175*
    Homemade Pickles, **157,** 174
    Panino Cubano, 153, 156, 157, 158, **174,** *175*
pie plates, *123*
pizza
    Basic Pizza Dough, **117-18,** 119, 120, 126, 128,
        129, 132, 133, 134, 136
    Cauliflower Pizza, **128-29**
    Celery Root Pizza, **133**
    Fennel Pizza, **140**
    freezing dough for, 117
    Mushroom Pizza, **126,** *127*
    Onion Pizza, **134,** *135*
    Pizza Amatriciana, **121**
    Pizza Batata, **130**
    Pizza Bianca, *114, 136,* **137-39**
    Pizza Cavolfiore, **128-29**
    Pizza Cipolla, **134,** 135
    Pizza Finocchio, **140**
    Pizza Funghi, **126,** *127,* 128
    Pizza Patate, **129-30, 131**
    Pizza Pomodoro, **120-21,** *121*
    Pizza Radici di Sedano, **133**
    Pizza Zucchine, **132**

Potato Pizza, **129-30,** *131*
Schicciata D'Uva, **139**
slicing, 122
Sweet Potato Pizza, **130**
Sweet Raisin and Grape Pizza, **139**
Tomato Pizza, **120-21,** *121*
Zucchini Pizza, **132**
Pizza Amatriciana, **121**
Pizza Batata, **130**
Pizza Bianca, *114, 136,* **137-39**
Pizza Cavolfiore, **128-29**
Pizza Cipolla, **134,** *135*
pizza cutters, *124*
Pizza Finocchio, **140**
Pizza Funghi, **126,** 127, 128
Pizza Patate, **129-30,** *131*
Pizza Pomodoro, **120-21,** *121*
Pizza Radici di Sedano, **133**
Pizza Zucchine, **132**
pizza stones, *123*
pizza wheels, 122
plastic spatulas, *123*
pork. *See also* pancetta; prosciutto cotto;
        prosciutto di Parma; speck
    Citrus Roast Pork, **152-53,** *153, 155,* 174
    Cuban Sandwich, 153, 156, 157, 158, **174,** *175*
    Panino Cubano, 153, 156, 157, 158, **174,** *175*
pot(s), 42, 45
potatoes
    Focaccia, **141-42,** *143*
    Frittata Patate, **170-71,** 186
    Pizza Batata, *130*
    Pizza Patate, **129-30,** *131*
    Potato Omelette, **170-71**
    Potato Pizza, **129-30,** *131*
    Sweet Potato Pizza, **130**
Potato Omelette, **170-71**
Potato Pizza, **129-30, 131**
prosciutto cotto
    Mozzarella Sandwich with Eggplant Spread,
        166, **179**
    Panino di Mozzarella, 166, **179**
prosciutto di Parma
    Cuban Sandwich, 153, 156, 157, 158, **174,**
        175
    Panino Cubano, 153, 156, 157, 158, **174,** *175*
protective gloves, 125

R

racks, *44, 124*

raisins
Fennel-Raisin Bread, **112-13,** 140
Focaccia Dolce, **144-45**
Pan co' Santi, **66-67,** *67*
Schicciata D'Uva, **139**
Sweet Focaccia, **144-45**
Sweet Raisin and Grape Pizza, **139**
Walnut Bread, **66-67,** *67*

Ramp Bagna Cauda, **169**
"Rampwich," 169, **184-85**
Ribollita, **198-99**
rising of dough, 41, 50-51

roast(s)
Citrus Roast Pork, **152-53,** *153, 155,* 174
Rosemary Roast Beef, 149, **150-51,** 173
tying, 154

Roast Beef Sandwich with Aioli, 151, 156, *163,*
164, **173**
Roasted Red Pepper Bruschetta, **202,** *203*
Roasted Red Peppers, **165**

rolls
Banana Leaf Rolls, **87-88,** *89*
Pancetta Rolls, **74,** *75*

romano beans
Ribollita, *188,* **198-99**
Thick Tuscan Bean and Kale Soup, *188,*
198-99

Römertopf Clay Baker, 81, *83*
Römertopf French Bread Baker, 79, 80
Rosemary Roast Beef, 149, **150-51,** 173
rubber spatulas, *43*
Rye Bread, **63-64,** *65*

S

salad
Bread Salad, **192-93**
Panzanella, **192-93**
salt, *123*
yeast activity and, 41
sandwiches, 149-87
Artichoke and Ham Sandwich, 160, **176**
Beet Sandwich with Goat Cheese, 163, **181**

Cuban Sandwich, 153, 156, 157, 158, **174,** *175*
Dried Beef Sandwich with Arugula, 167, **180**
Eggplant Sandwich with Roasted Red
Pepper, 161, 165, **178**
Green Onion Bagna Cauda, Mozzarella, and
Duck Egg Sandwich, 169, **184-85**
Mozzarella and Tomato Sandwich, **177,** 179
Mozzarella Sandwich with Eggplant Spread,
166, **179**
Omelette Sandwich, 171, **186,** *187*
Pancetta, Mango, and Basil Sandwich, 149,
182, *183*
Panino Cubano, 153, 156, 157, 158, **174,** *175*
Panino de Barbietola, 163, **181**
Panino di Bresaola, *163,* 167, **180**
Panino di Caprese, **177,** 179
Panino di Carciofi e Prosciutto Cotto, 160, **176**
Panino di Manzo, 151, 156, *163,* 164, **173**
Panino di Melanzane, 149, 161, 165, **178**
Panino di Mozzarella, 166, **179**
Panino Frittata, 171, **186,** 187
Panino "PMB," 149, **182,** *183*
"Rampwich," 169, **184-85**
Roast Beef Sandwich with Aioli, 151, 156, *163,*
164, **173**
"Speckeroni," *146,* 164, 166, **185**
Speck with Pecorino Sandwich, *146,* 164, 166,
185
sandwich ingredients
Artichoke Confit, **159-60,** 176
Citrus Roast Pork, **152-53,** *153, 155,* 174
Frittata Patate, **170-71**
Green Onion, Anchovy, and Garlic Sauce,
168-69
Green Onion Bagna Cauda, **168-69,** 184
Homemade Pickles, **157,** 174
Homemade Spicy Mustard, **158,** 174
Jim's Aioli, **156,** 173, 174, 186
Lemon Dressing, **167**
Marinated Beets, **163-64**
Marinated Eggplant, **160-61,** 166
Marinated Sun-Dried Tomatoes, **164,** 166,
173
Potato Omelette, **170-71**
Ramp Bagna Cauda, **169**
Roasted Red Peppers, **165**
Rosemary Roast Beef, 149, **150-51,** 173

Spicy Eggplant Spread, **166,** 179, 185
Savoy cabbage
　Ribollita, *188,* **198-99**
　Thick Tuscan Bean and Kale Soup, *188,*
　　198-99
scales, *43*
Schicciata D'Uva, **139**
seawater
　Jones Beach Bread, **90-91**
　Ocean Bread with Nori, **91**
seaweed
　Ocean Bread with Nori, **91**
Shun mandolines, 125
singing, *47*
slicing
　bread, 42, 47
　ingredients, 12, 125
　pizza, 122
Slipper Loaf, **81-82,** *83*
soups
　Gazpacho, **196-97**
　Pappa al Pomodoro, **194-95**
　Ribollita, *188,* **198-99**
　Thick Tuscan Bean and Kale Soup, *188,*
　　198-99
　Tomato Bread Soup, **194-95**
spatulas
　plastic, *123*
　rubber, *43*
speck
　"Speckeroni," *146, 164, 166,* **185**
　Speck with Pecorino Sandwich, *146, 164, 166,*
　　185
Spicy Eggplant Spread, **166,** 179, 185
spoons
　measuring, *43*
　wooden, *43, 124*
spreads
　Mozzarella Sandwich with Eggplant Spread,
　　166, **179**
　Spicy Eggplant Spread, **166,** 179, 185
steam, 41-42
Stecca, *56, 76,* **77-78,** *77,* 172, 173, 174, 176, 177,
　178, 179, 180, 181, 182, 184, 186
Stecca Pomodori, All'Olive, O Al'Aglio, **78**
Stecca with Tomatoes, Olives, or Garlic, **78**
Stick (small baguette), *56, 76,* **77-78,** 172, 173,

　174, 176, 177, 178, 179, 180, 181, 182, 184,
　186
Stirato, **79-80,** 172, 173, 174, 175, 176, 177, 178,
　179, 180, 181, 182, 184, 185, 186
storing bread, 49
Sullivan Street Bakery, 31-33, *169*
Sweet Focaccia, **144-45**
sweet potatoes
　Pizza Batata, **130**
　Sweet Potato Pizza, **130**
Sweet Raisin and Grape Pizza, **139**
Swiss cheese
　Pizza Zucchine, **132**
　Zucchini Pizza, **132**

T

tarts
　Bread Pudding Tart, **204-6**
　Budino, **204-6,** 207
tea towels, *44*
Thick Tuscan Bean and Kale Soup, *188,*
　198-99
timer, *44*
timing, 50-51
　in very cold weather, 51
tomato(es)
　basil, **177**
　Bread Salad, **192-93**
　Gazpacho, **196-97**
　Marinated Sun-Dried Tomatoes, **164,** 166,
　　173
　Mozzarella and Tomato Sandwich, **177,**
　　179
　Neapolitan Tomato Bruschetta, **201**
　Panino di Caprese, **177,** 179
　Panzanella, **192-93**
　Pappa al Pomodoro, **194-95**
　Pizza Amatriciana, **121**
　Pizza Pomodoro, **120-21,** *121*
　Ribollita, *188,* **198-99**
　Stecca Pomodori, All'Olive, O Al'Aglio, **78**
　Stecca with Tomatoes, Olives, or Garlic, **78**
　Thick Tuscan Bean and Kale Soup, *188,*
　　198-99
　Tomato Bread Soup, **194-95**

tomato(es) (*continued*)
    Tomato Bruschetta, **200-201**
    Tomato Pizza, **120-21,** *121*
    Tomato Pizza with Pancetta and Onion, **121**
Tomato Bread Soup, **194-95**
Tomato Bruschetta, **200-201**
Tomato Pizza, **120-21,** 121
Tomato Pizza with Pancetta and Onions, **121**
torte
    Chocolate Torte, *208*, **209-10**
    Tortino di Cioccolato, *208*, **209-10**

W

walnut(s)
    Carrot Bread, *96*, **97-98**
    Pan co' Santi, **66-67,** *67*
    Walnut Bread, **66-67,** *67*
water, 92
    seawater, 90

weighing ingredients, 48
white wine
    Focaccia Dolce, **144-45**
    Sweet Focaccia, **144-45**
Whole Wheat Bread, *60*, **61-62**
whole wheat flour, 61
wooden spoons, *43, 124*

Y

yeast, 40-41

Z

zucchini
    Pizza Zucchine, **132**
    Zucchini Pizza, **132**

The Author in Pictures

Jim Lahey, master baker and founder of the Sullivan Street Bakery in New York City, is a dedicated innovator who passionately believes that ancient bread-making techniques can be interpreted for the modern kitchen. He is committed to redefining and elevating the standard of bread-making for professional and home bakers alike.

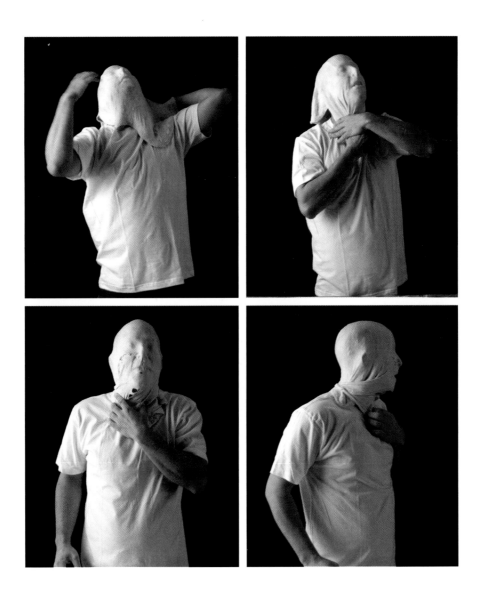